Al

Modern Internet Services

Alexander Totok

Modern Internet Services

Exploiting Service Usage Information for Optimizing Service Management

VDM Verlag Dr. Müller

Impressum/Imprint (nur für Deutschland/ only for Germany)
Bibliografische Information der Deutschen Nationalbibliothek: Die Deutsche Nationalbibliothek
verzeichnet diese Publikation in der Deutschen Nationalbibliografie; detaillierte bibliografische
Daten sind im Internet über http://dnb.d-nb.de abrufbar.
Alle in diesem Buch genannten Marken und Produktnamen unterliegen warenzeichen-, marken-
oder patentrechtlichem Schutz bzw. sind Warenzeichen oder eingetragene Warenzeichen der
jeweiligen Inhaber. Die Wiedergabe von Marken, Produktnamen, Gebrauchsnamen,
Handelsnamen, Warenbezeichnungen u.s.w. in diesem Werk berechtigt auch ohne besondere
Kennzeichnung nicht zu der Annahme, dass solche Namen im Sinne der Warenzeichen- und
Markenschutzgesetzgebung als frei zu betrachten wären und daher von jedermann benutzt
werden dürften.

Coverbild: www.purestockx.com

Verlag: VDM Verlag Dr. Müller Aktiengesellschaft & Co. KG
Dudweiler Landstr. 99, 66123 Saarbrücken, Deutschland
Telefon +49 681 9100-698, Telefax +49 681 9100-988, Email: info@vdm-verlag.de
Zugl.: New York, New York University, Dissertation, 2006

Herstellung in Deutschland:
Schaltungsdienst Lange o.H.G., Berlin
Books on Demand GmbH, Norderstedt
Reha GmbH, Saarbrücken
Amazon Distribution GmbH, Leipzig
ISBN: 978-3-639-15898-4

Imprint (only for USA, GB)
Bibliographic information published by the Deutsche Nationalbibliothek: The Deutsche
Nationalbibliothek lists this publication in the Deutsche Nationalbibliografie; detailed
bibliographic data are available in the Internet at http://dnb.d-nb.de.
Any brand names and product names mentioned in this book are subject to trademark, brand or
patent protection and are trademarks or registered trademarks of their respective holders. The use
of brand names, product names, common names, trade names, product descriptions etc. even
without a particular marking in this works is in no way to be construed to mean that such names
may be regarded as unrestricted in respect of trademark and brand protection legislation and
could thus be used by anyone.

Cover image: www.purestockx.com

Publisher:
VDM Verlag Dr. Müller Aktiengesellschaft & Co. KG
Dudweiler Landstr. 99, 66123 Saarbrücken, Germany
Phone +49 681 9100-698, Fax +49 681 9100-988, Email: info@vdm-publishing.com
New York, New York University, Dissertation, 2006

Printed in the U.S.A.
Printed in the U.K. by (see last page)
ISBN: 978-3-639-15898-4

Table of Contents

2

3

4

Chapter 1

Introduction

1.1 Motivation

In recent decade, the role of the Internet has undergone a transition from simply being a data repository to one providing access to a variety of network-accessible services such as e-mail, social networking, banking, on-line shopping, and entertainment. The emergence of these web portals has marked a shift from monolithically structured web sites giving access to static read-only content, which were typical for the early Internet, to complex distributed on-line services providing richer functionality, that dominate the modern Internet. These services experience several commonalities in the way they are structured and the way they are used by their clients:

- **Session-oriented usage by clients.** Typical interaction of users with such services is organized into *sessions*, a sequence of related requests, which together achieve a higher level user goal. An example of such interaction is an on-line shopping scenario for an e-Commerce web site, which involves multiple requests that search for particular products, retrieve information about a specific item (e.g., quantity and price), add it to the shopping cart, initiate the check-out process, and finally commit the order. The *success of the whole session* now becomes the ultimate client's goal, which contrasts with *per-request success* performance metrics of the early Internet.

- **Complex data access patterns.** Application data no longer has *read-only* access, as was typical for the older content-providing web sites. In the scenarios such as one mentioned above, certain service requests not only read, but also *write* application data. Moreover, concurrent requests coming from different clients can access and modify *shared* application data. The data is no longer static, but is rather dynamically processed and assembled from the pieces obtained from the data storages, before being sent to the client. The data access patterns get even more complicated when the application data is replicated (e.g., for failover purposes) or partitioned (e.g., due to business requirements). The outcome and the complexity of a request execution may depend on the datasources it accesses and may get influenced by the execution of concurrent user requests, which may change shared application data accessed in the session. For some services, it becomes crucial to preserve the *correctness* of a session's execution, with regards to the data it accesses.

- **Use of component middleware.** A growing number of service providers are utilizing increasingly popular commercial-off-the-shelf (COTS) component middleware as a platform for building their services. Such services are structured as aggregations of multiple components communicating with each other and with the back-end datasources, while the middleware provides commonly required support for communication, security, persistence, clustering and transactions. Current-day industry standard component frameworks, exemplified by OMG's CORBA Component Model [95], Sun Microsystems' Java Platform Enterprise Edition (Java EE) [121] and Microsoft's .NET [92] frameworks significantly reduce the effort it takes to design, implement, deploy, maintain, and upgrade applications. Because of the application modular structure and the fact that the middleware takes responsibility to provide some of the functionality, an application's behavior depends not only on the way it is programmed, but also on the way it is assembled, deployed, and managed at run-time. As an example, changing middleware policies such as transaction demarcation may significantly impact not only application *performance*, but

6

also certain aspects of application *logic* and the correctness of data, presented to its users. This makes *application assemblers, application deployers*, and *system administrators*, equally with *application developers*, responsible for the behavior of component-based Internet services.

These characteristics have implications for how one ensures reasonable service quality for client requests against such services. Inadequate performance and sporadic incorrect behavior of an Internet service leads to user frustration, and as a consequence, to lowered usage of the service and reduced revenues. Providing good *performance Quality of Service (QoS)* has been a classical problem for web site providers, however, the characteristics outlined above have made this problem even harder. Not only providing any performance guarantees is affected by the increased implementation and structural complexity of modern Internet services, but the service provider now also needs to take care of insuring correctness of *service (application) logic* and providing expected *data quality* to the service clients.

Performance quality. The survey in [61] showed that around 19% of the people surveyed attribute to bad performance the bad experiences they had with Internet services. The primary performance concern for Internet service users is *request response time* [104]. According to some estimates, in 1998 alone about 10 – 25% of e-Commerce transactions were aborted owing to long response delays, which translated to about 1.9 billion dollars loss of revenue [143].

The response delay of Internet service is determined by two factors: the quality of network transmission and the processing capacity of the server. With the rapid Internet expansion and the client base moving away from the slow dial-up connections, more and more users nowadays have fast access to the Internet, which makes the server-side request processing time typically a dominant factor in the overall response delay. Therefore, fast execution of requests at the server side has become the key factor in providing user perceivable performance. This is especially true in a situation of service *overload*, when user load nears or exceeds the server capacity, which causes request rejections and increases request response times, even

7

in absence of network disruptions.

To improve server performance in the situation of high load or overload, service providers have traditionally used server-side resource management mechanisms to *improve utilization of server resources*. But this is harder to do for modern Internet services, for the following three main reasons. First, component middleware usually exposes to service providers (more precisely, to system administrators) several mechanisms that can be independently tuned in attempt to improve server performance and optimize server resource utilization. Such mechanisms include, for example, thread and component pool management, data caching and request scheduling strategies. These mechanisms do not provide a unique server configuration, which would be optimal for all request loads. Second, more complex session-oriented client behavior makes it hard to predict what impact tuning of a certain server resource management mechanism would bring on the server performance, which may vary for different incoming request mixes. Finally, modern component-based applications exhibit complex structural organization, where different sets of application components and middleware services are used to execute requests of different types. Some requests, for example, may need to access a back-end database, some may need CPU-intensive processing, while some may need exclusive access to a component or a critical resource.

Inability of service providers to predict the exact effects of using the server resource management mechanisms on server performance for a given client load structure accounts for the fact that these mechanisms are often used in an "ad-hoc" or a "best-guess" manner. This results in suboptimal usage of server resources, not tailored for specific incoming request load, and, as a consequence, the service clients not getting the best performance quality they potentially could get.

Service logic and data quality. Clients of an Internet service reasonably expect that the service operates according to the advertised functionality, presents valid information, correctly processes and stores the data submitted by its users. It is generally perceived that such correctness of the *service (application) logic* is solely the responsibility of the application developers.

However, this may not hold true for modern complex component-based applications, which are often assembled from third-party components, and where some application functionality is delegated to the middleware. The behavior of this latter functionality is guided by additional information provided by application assemblers, application deployers and system administrators (through so-called deployment descriptors and run-time application server policies). This information and run-time policies may significantly impact the application behavior and the quality of data presented to its users, in a worst case scenario even resulting in a critically incorrect or abnormal application execution.

An example of such an undesired service behavior is so-called "fare jumping," when in a shopping session scenario an item's price increases between the time a client first looks at it and the time he tries to checkout the order. A recent report showed that such an issue presents a problem for the e-Commerce web sites selling airline tickets [128]. Such *data quality* problems stem from several facts. First, client requests read and write shared application data, potentially invalidating the data accessed by concurrent requests of different users. Second, the application data gets cached and replicated, which results in some requests returning out-of-date or invalid information.

A typical approach to cope with these problems is for application developers to try to retain as much control over application functionality and data manipulation as possible in the application code. Another approach, employed by service providers, is to minimize the extent to which concurrent execution of user sessions is allowed. Similarly, data replication or distribution (e.g., for performance purposes), might be limited (by employing extra "guardian" mechanisms, e.g., in additional application functionality), which prevents undesired execution scenarios, but often also eliminates or diminishes the benefits brought by the service replication or distribution in the first place.

However, both of these approaches seem to be inadequate. First, they contradict with the very concept and the nature of component middleware, where as much functionality as possible is offloaded from the applications to the middleware. Second, they place an unnatural burden on applica-

9

tion developers, limit application modularity and reuse, and undermine the potential for application evolution. And third, they worsen the service performance or restrict the usage of the service by its clients.

In order to provide reasonable service logic and data quality guarantees, while not limiting service performance, service providers need to precisely understand how the data-quality-affecting server-side mechanisms they employ (e.g., transaction demarcation, data caching and replication) impact the application logic and the quality of application data. On the other hand, the application developers need some guidelines for application development and structuring that would enable efficient use of these middleware mechanisms.

1.2   Approach and methodology

In this book, we focus on solutions that target the three interconnected goals described above: (1) providing improved QoS guarantees to the clients of Internet services; (2) achieving optimal server resource management and utilization by the service providers; and (3) provide the application developers with the guidelines for natural application structuring, that enable efficient use of the state-of-the-art mechanisms for improving service performance. Specifically, we make the claim that **exposing and using detailed information about how clients use component-based Internet services enables mechanisms that achieve the range of goals listed above.** The techniques that we describe and evaluate in this book take into account various aspects of service usage by clients and are applicable at both the *application structuring* stage and the *application operation* stage.

Service usage (or service access) information can be exposed at different levels — from high-level structure of user sessions, to low level information about resource consumption by different request types. Some of this information can be automatically obtained by request profiling, some can be obtained by statically analyzing the application structure, while some needs to be specified by the service provider. In this book, we identify four related groups of *service access attributes*, that correspond to different levels of service usage information. The relationship between different service

10

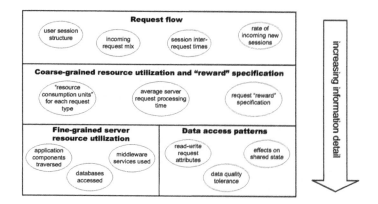

Figure 1.1: Relationship between the service access attributes.

access attributes is schematically shown in Fig. 1.1.

1. **Request flow.** This service access attribute provides the coarse-grain-ed information about the requests that are being invoked against the service. The information about an individual service request is lim-ited to its type, session (client) identity, and (optionally) the time of its arrival. Such information may come in different forms. For exam-ple, it may state the rate and the arrival pattern of the requests of a certain type as they are received by the server. Alternatively, it may come in the form of a client session structure specification. Request flow information may contain various timing parameters, such as ses-sion inter-request times, or the rate of incoming new sessions. The information provided by the request flow service access attribute rep-resents the highest level of service usage information, and usually can be obtained through real-time profiling of incoming client requests.

2. **Coarse-grained resource utilization and "reward".** This service access attribute contains information about high-level "cost" of exe-

11

cution of requests of different types. This information can help on an approximate comparison of resource consumption by different request types, and can be either specified by the service provider in the form of abstract *resource consumption units* or determined by average request processing times. In the latter case it can be automatically obtained through request profiling. The service provider may also specify so-called "reward" (or "profit") brought by each type of service request. This is an opportunity for providers of business critical services to indicate which requests are more valuable, according to the service logic, or to indicate which requests are crucial for the service in bringing the profit.

3. **Fine-grained server resource utilization.** This service access attribute provides more detailed information about service requests of different types. It contains the information about how requests are processed in the application server. It may specify what application components are traversed or what middleware services are used in the execution of a request. It may also indicate what databases a request needs to access, in what order, and how long the request spends in each of the databases, on average. The actual information about the way a request gets processed by the server varies for different problems, QoS targets and metrics being optimized. Information of such flavor can be obtained through a fine-grained profiling of server-side request processing or, in some cases, by statically analyzing the application code structure.

4. **Data access patterns.** This service access attribute contains the information about how requests access application data. It may specify whether a request is read-only, read-write, or write-only. It may specify what segments of application data are accessed during the execution of a request, whether this data is shared among several clients or not, and what are the consequences of accessing this data. It may also specify how tolerable a certain request to *application data quality* — this information may be used in managing data replication and caching. While a request's read-write data access patterns can be ob-

tained through request profiling or static code analysis, such information as the tolerance to application data quality needs to be specified by the service provider, based on some external business or QoS requirements, not "encoded" in the application structure or logic.

To validate the claim that service usage information can be used to improve QoS guarantees and to better manage Internet services, we show its applicability to the following four problems: **(1) maximizing reward brought by Internet services, (2) optimizing utilization of server resource pools, (3) providing session data integrity guarantees, and (4) enabling service distribution in wide-area environments.**

The problems were chosen to represent a wide range of challenges that service providers face in operating modern Internet services. In each problem we show how utilizing specific service access attributes helps to achieve the problem goal. Not all of the service access attributes are equally useful for all problems, which utilize different kinds of service usage information (see Table 1.1) and exhibit different amounts of automatic exploitation of such information. The solutions and techniques described in each problem differ, but they span a representative range of mechanisms that researchers have proposed and used for predicting and improving performance of Internet services and server resource utilization. These mechanisms and techniques include: analytical modeling, statistical methods (event profiling and information gathering, Bayesian inference analysis), resource management mechanisms (admission control, request prioritization and scheduling, concurrency control techniques), and application restructuring.

All of the described mechanisms, except for application restructuring, can be implemented in a modular and pluggable fashion as middleware services, which makes possible their voluntary use that does not require changing the original application code of Internet services. We present these mechanisms in a centralized setting for simplicity, in order to concentrate on the essence of the described techniques. We expect that these mechanisms can be successfully scaled, and that their benefits will be also visible in a distributed setting. The application restructuring techniques, on the contrary, are presented only in a distributed setting, where their use,

Table 1.1: Service access attributes used by the problems addressed in the book.

	Request flow	Coarse-grained resource utilization and reward	Fine-grained resource utilization	Data access patterns
Maximizing reward brought by Internet services	X	X		
Optimizing utilization of server resource pools	X		X	
Session data integrity guarantees	X			X
Enabling service distribution in wide area			X	X

as we demonstrate it, is absolutely necessary in order to improve service performance. Application restructuring mechanisms can be also used in a centralized setting, but their contribution in the overall QoS improvement here is not so prominent — most of the benefits can be achieved through the described server resource management mechanisms.

We describe the four problems addressed in this book in more detail below.

1.2.1 Maximizing reward brought by Internet services

In a typical setting a web application server hosting an Internet service processes the incoming user request on a first-come-first-served basis. This approach provides fair access to the service for all clients. When a need emerges to provide some clients with a better service (e.g., based on their predefined customer status), the request scheduling and processing is governed by Service Level Agreements (SLA) or other analogous mechanisms that differentiate between different client groups. A common element in all these schemes is that QoS received by a client is determined upfront by its association with a client group.

While trying to provide its clients with reasonable or prenegotiated QoS, the service provider running a commercial service also wants to boost its revenues. Different user sessions bring different profit to the service provider. For example, in the on-line shopping scenario introduced earlier, the service provider might be interested in giving a higher execution priority to the sessions that end up *buying* something (*buyer* sessions), and a lower priority — to the sessions that don't buy anything (*browser* sessions), making sure that clients that buy something receive better QoS. However, the information about user intentions to buy products is not encoded in its client group's profile, so SLA-based approaches are not as beneficial here.

To be able to provide better QoS to the sessions that *bring more profit (reward)*, the service provider needs tools to *predict* the future behavior of a session based on the sessions's requests seen so far. The thesis we explore in this problem is that information about how clients used the service in the recent past may help in such prediction, if the service usage patterns do not change rapidly. In this book, we describe *reward-driven request prioritization* schemes that use this information to assign higher priority to the sessions that are likely to give more reward. The mechanisms, which are seamlessly integrated into the middleware platform, work in an application-independent manner, based on the information exposed by the *coarse-grained resource utilization and reward* service access attribute. They also automatically obtain (through request profiling) and use the information about the request structure of user sessions.

The mechanisms provide several benefits. In the situation of service *underload* they give better response times to clients that bring more profit (reward) to the service, which is a crucial thing for keeping the customers satisfied and ensuring that they will return to the service.[1] In the situation of

---

[1] Several independent studies have shown that the bulk of a service's clients are returning clients,

service *overload*, when some of the requests get rejected, the mechanisms ensure that sessions that bring more reward are more likely to complete successfully and that the profit attained by the service increases compared to other solutions, such as fair session-based admission control (SBAC).

1.2.2   Optimizing utilization of server resource pools

Modern component middleware are complex software systems that expose to service providers several mechanisms that can be independently tuned in attempt to improve server performance and optimize server resource utilization. Middleware itself rarely has control over low-level OS mechanisms, such as CPU scheduling and memory management. It rather provides control over higher-level resources, such as threads, database connections, component containers, etc. Some of these resources can be shared among concurrent client requests, but some are *held exclusively by a request* for the duration of its execution (or a part of it). Therefore, such non-shared resources become *bottleneck points*, and failure to obtain such a resource constitutes a major portion of request rejections under high load or overload conditions. Optimizing utilization of these resources (among which the most important are threads and database connections) becomes a high priority goal for the service provider. However, this task proves to be nontrivial, because for different client loads different configurations of the thread and database (DB) connection pools provide the optimal performance. This happens because different sets of application components and middleware services are used to execute requests of different types. Some requests need to access a database (so they need to obtain and exclusively hold a DB connection), while some don't.

To come up with a solution to this problem, we present and use a model of request execution with a 2-tier exclusive resource holding (1st tier — threads, 2nd tier — DB connections). This model uses the information about *fine-grained server resource utilization*, obtained through an instrumented request profiling in a limited set of off-line experiments, where the actual server environment is subjected to an artificial client load. Under

---

and that providing good QoS to long-time clients is a key factor in a service success [97, 137].

16

the real operation conditions, the model takes as input the *request flow* information, obtained through on-line request profiling, and computes the configuration of the thread and DB connection pools, which provides the best request throughput, for a given mix of incoming client requests, thus achieving the optimal utilization of web server threads and DB connections.

1.2.3 Session data integrity guarantees

This problem deals with the previously described situation of ensuring *application data quality*, when multiple concurrent user sessions involve requests that read and write shared application state and potentially invalidate each other's data. Depending on the nature of the business represented by the service, allowing the session with invalid data to progress might lead to financial penalties for the service provider, while blocking the session's progress and deferring its execution (e.g., by relaying its handling to human) will most probably result in user dissatisfaction. A compromise would be to tolerate some *bounded data inconsistency*, which would allow most of the sessions to progress, while limiting the potential financial loss incurred by the service. In order to quantitatively reason about these trade-offs, the service provider can benefit from models that predict metrics, such as the percentage of successfully completed sessions, for a certain degree of tolerable data inconsistency.

In this book, we describe analytical models of concurrent web sessions with bounded inconsistency in shared data for three popular concurrency control algorithms. The models operate in an application-independent manner using abstract data access model. Mapping of service requests to the operations of this model is done by the service provider, who uses the information about application *data access patterns*, to identify how service requests access and change shared application state. The described analytical models take as input *request flow* information obtained through real-time profiling of incoming client requests. We illustrate the models using the sample buyer scenario for an on-line store and validate them by showing their close correspondence to measured results of concurrent session execution in both a simulated and a real web server environment. We also show that a middleware server environment with an added automated de-

17

cision making mechanism can successfully choose, based on the specified performance metric, the best concurrency control algorithm in real time in response to changing service usage patterns.

1.2.4   Service distribution in wide-area environments

Application distribution and replication has recently become a noticeable trend in the way modern Internet services are designed and utilized. These techniques bring application data and data processing *closer to the clients* and help to cope, on the network level, with unpredictable nature of Internet traffic, especially in wide-area environments, and, on the application level, with high-volume, widely varying, disparate client workloads.

Though nominally suitable for deployment in distributed environments, component-based applications are traditionally deployed only in a centralized fashion in high-performance local area networks. In the rare cases when these applications are distributed in wide-area environments, the systems tend to be highly customized and handcrafted. When a general component application is distributed in wide area environments, inter-component communication, otherwise "invisible" in local area networks, becomes a key factor in dramatically increased request response times, which eliminates the benefits of application distribution in the first place.

For an application distributed in wide area environments, response time of a request significantly depends on what components and back-end data-sources are accessed during its execution. Information of this kind belongs to the *fine-grained resource utilization* service access attribute and needs to be available for the service provider to be able to assess performance quality of a distributed application. On the other hand, in order to ensure that popular or business critical service requests experience small response delays, the application should be engineered in a way that limits unnecessary wide area inter-component communication. To achieve this, the application developer needs to be aware of (1) the "read-write" data access behavior of service requests; and (2) whether the application state accessed in a request is shared among several clients or not. In other words, while developing the application, one needs to take into account the application *data access patterns*.

18

In this book, we identify and recommend for use a small set of *design rules for application development and construction*, that enable beneficial and efficient service distribution in wide area environments. We validate the applicability of the described design rules by applying them to several sample component-based applications and showing performance benefits of their wide area distributed deployments.

1.3 Contributions

The high-level contribution of this work is a set of models, techniques, middleware mechanisms, and application design rules, showing that exposing and using detailed information about session-oriented usage of component-based Internet services by their clients helps to (1) improve QoS delivered to the clients; (2) optimize server resource management and utilization; and (3) provide the application developers with the guidelines for natural application structuring that enable efficient use of the state-of-the-art mechanisms for improving service performance.

Specifically, the contributions of this work are the following:

Models and techniques.

- Reward-driven session prioritization schemes, which show their utility for improving the QoS delivered to users that bring the most profit to the Internet service, and for maximizing profit attained by the service in the overload situations.

- A model of request execution with 2-tier exclusive server resource holding (threads, database connections), which enables accurate prediction of the optimal configuration for the thread and database connection pools in component application servers, for a given mix of client requests.

- Analytical models of concurrent web session execution with bounded inconsistency in shared application data, which are able to accurately predict the values of QoS metrics of interest.

19

Middleware mechanisms.

- Middleware request profiling infrastructure, which permits one to obtain service usage information at different levels without imposing significant performance overheads.

- A set of middleware decision-making mechanisms (e.g., request prioritization, automatic concurrency control for web sessions, etc.), implemented in a modular, extensible, and pluggable fashion with minimal, backward compatible, changes to the original web application server code. These mechanisms show their effectiveness in making run-time resource-utilization decisions and in determining the optimal configuration of critical server resources, without significant performance and management overheads. We have implemented and evaluated the mechanisms in a production-level application server JBoss [68], which utilizes the Java EE component model [121]. However, we believe that the described techniques and mechanisms are general enough to be applicable to web servers utilizing other technologies.

Application design rules.

- A set of application design rules that enable beneficial and efficient distribution of component-based Internet services in wide area environments.

Different parties involved in different stages of a component-based Internet service lifecycle could benefit from different aspects of the work presented in this book. Application developers could benefit from using the described set of application design rules and optimizations for building component-based applications. Middleware architects and developers could benefit from utilizing the set of described middleware mechanisms to introduce their functionality into the middleware systems. Service operators (e.g., system administrators) could benefit from using the described models and techniques in order to boost performance of component-based

20

Internet services and improve their manageability, given that these mechanisms and the corresponding functionality is provided by the underlying middleware.

1.4 Book organization

Chapter 2 provides necessary background information. It gives a short introduction into the area of component frameworks and applications, and specifically acquaints the reader with the Java EE component middleware [121]. Then it discusses previous research efforts and work related to this study in the areas of web workload modeling, Internet server performance, transaction processing and service distribution. Chapter 3 describes in greater detail the four identified *service access attributes*, and how this information is obtained and abstracted into specific models of service usage and resource utilization, used in this work. The four problems (Sections 1.2.1 through 1.2.4), chosen to validate the main claim made in this book, and the described solutions, mechanisms, and techniques are separately described in Chapters 4, 5, 6, and 7. The book ends with Chapter 8, where we present conclusions and identify interesting directions for future research.

Chapter 2

Background and Related Work

The work focuses on Internet-accessible services implemented using component frameworks. First, we give some background on component frameworks in general and the Java EE platform in particular, briefly describe the structure of the JBoss application server, and introduce sample Java EE applications used in this study. Then, we discuss research efforts relevant to the work presented in this book, in the areas of web workload characterization, performance of Internet services, transaction processing, and service distribution.

2.1 Component frameworks

Component software. Traditional software development strategies can broadly be divided into two camps. At one extreme, a project is developed entirely from scratch, with the help of only programming tools and libraries. At the other extreme, everything is "outsourced", in other words, standard software is bought and parameterized to provide a solution that is "close enough" to what is needed.

The concept of *component software* [126] represents the middle path, where the entire application is *assembled* from individual components, developed by third parties. Although each component is a standardized product, with all the advantages that brings, the process of component assembly allows the opportunity for significant customization, thus avoiding the

22

drawbacks of using standard monolithic software applications. In addition, some individual components can be custom-made to suit specific requirements or to foster strategic advantages.

Component frameworks. In its early days most of the emphasis in the development of component software was on the construction of individual components and on the basic "wiring" support of components, leading to specifications such as Java RMI [122] and COM/DCOM [91]. It was highly unlikely that components developed independently under such conditions would be able to cooperate usefully.

The inception of *component frameworks* was the most important step that lifted component software off the ground. A component framework is a software system that supports components conforming to certain standards and allows instances of these components to be "plugged" into the component framework. The component framework establishes environmental conditions for the components and regulates the interactions between them. This is usually done through *containers*, component holders, which often also provide commonly required support for naming, security, transactions, and persistence. Component frameworks provide an integrated environment for component execution, as a result significantly reducing the effort it takes to design, implement, deploy, and maintain applications. Current day industry component framework standards are represented by Object Management Group's CORBA Component Model [95], Sun Microsystems' Java Platform Enterprise Edition (Java EE) [121] and Microsoft's .NET [92], with Java EE being currently the most popular and widely used component framework in the enterprise arena.

2.2   Java Platform Enterprise Edition

Java Platform Enterprise Edition (Java EE) [121] (formerly known as Java 2 Platform Enterprise Edition — J2EE) is the widely accepted industry-level component framework introduced by Sun Microsystems, based on the Java programming language.

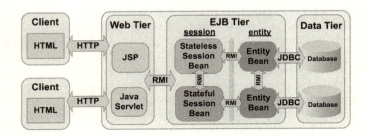

Figure 2.1: Java EE component architecture.

2.2.1 3-tier architecture

Applications developed using the Java EE framework adhere to the classical 3-tier architecture — *web tier*, *business tier*, and *data tier* (see Fig. 2.1). Java EE components belonging to each tier are developed adhering to specific Java EE standards.

Web tier. This tier deals with the presentation logic of the application. Components in this tier include *Java Servlets* [123] and *Java Server Pages (JSP)* [124]. These components are invoked to process incoming HTTP requests, and are responsible for the generation of the response HTML pages, invoking components from the business tier, or communicating directly with the data tier, to get application data from back-end datasources, if necessary. Java Servlets and JSPs are stateful components and hold HTTP session information.

Business tier. This tier, which is sometimes called *middle tier* or, in the Java EE realm, also — *EJB tier*, consists of *Enterprise Java Beans (EJB)* components [114], which have three flavors: *Session*, *Entity*, and *Message Driven*. Session beans usually provide generic application-wide services, and also serve as façade objects in front of shared persistent datasources. They are either stateless or instantiated to contain application state on a per-session basis. Stateful components holding session state (i.e., stateful session EJBs and web tier components) effectively act as an extension of the client's run-time environment on the server-side. Entity beans are transactional shared persistent entities, representing a synchronized in-memory copy of the database information. Message driven beans are stateless components and serve the purpose of processing incoming asynchronous JMS [118] messages.

Data tier. This tier serves the purpose of persistently storing the application data and is usually represented by relational databases. Java EE application components communicate with relational datasources through JDBC (Java DataBase Connectivity) [125] interfaces, or through other persistence mechanisms, such as Java Data Objects (JDO) [116].

2.2.2 Service request execution and inter-component communication

Clients usually communicate with Internet-accessible services through the HTTP protocol. Although HTTP is a stateless protocol, client identity is usually maintained with the help of *HTTP cookies* that are sent forth and back in every subsequent client request. The HTTP/web server keeps track of currently active user sessions. Upon arrival of an HTTP request at the web server, it is served by the corresponding Java Servlet or a (set of) JSP(s), as specified in the application configuration files. These Java Servlets and JSPs may, based on the application logic, trigger invocations of EJB (middle tier) components, which in turn may invoke other EJB components and access appropriate back-end datasources.

Components communicate with each other in a synchronous "request-reply" fashion (except for sending and receiving JMS messages), by invoking an appropriate components' business methods. Entity beans are usually synchronized with the corresponding database entities (an Entity bean usually corresponds to a row in a database table) using JDBC. Most of the application servers simplify this synchronization process by automatically generating the JDBC code, based on the information from the so-called *deployment descriptor(s)* — configuration files that among other things specify mapping of an entity beans' persistent fields to the database schema. However, all components may directly communicate with the database using JDBC.

Java EE components never invoke each other directly, as simple Java objects do. Application programmers specify component references in deployment descriptors by providing only the type (interface) and the JNDI (Java Naming and Directory Interface) [119] name of the referenced component. To make a component invocation, the invoking component first obtains a remote stub of the referenced component by performing a JNDI lookup and then invokes a business method on it. Before delegating the execution of a method to the referenced component object, the component container may, for example, need to update component's state (i.e., synchronize it with the database), or to activate the component (if it was passivated after a long period of inactivity). Therefore, the executed request first comes through several client- and server-side *proxies*, or *interceptors*, which are responsible for handling various aspects of the method invocation, such as security, transactions, persistence, etc. And only then is the requested method invoked on the target component object.

Some level of indirection also takes place when components communicate with relational databases. A common way to integrate relational back-end datasources into Java EE application servers is through the Java Connector Architecture (JCA) [115], which defines a set of scalable, secure, and transactional mechanisms for the integration of Enterprise Information Systems (EIS) with application servers. Using JCA allows the application server to pool database (DB) connections (for scalability purposes) and to manage their transactional and security aspects in a standardized fashion. To access a database, a component performs a JNDI lookup for a special JCA adaptor object, which, upon request, supplies the component with a wrapper object containing the actual DB connection taken from the pool. When the component "closes" the connection wrapper object, the physical DB connection is returned to the pool. This pooling mechanism allows one to avoid expensive operations of creating and closing DB connections.

The same idea of *resource pooling* for scalability and enhanced performance is also used by most HTTP/web servers in their pooling of server threads, which are also quite expensive to create and destroy.

2.2.3 Resource consumption and performance bottlenecks in Java EE applications

There are several aspects of application structuring and particulars of the Java EE middleware platform, which influence the performance of Java EE applications.

Component invocations. As the discussion in the previous section has suggested, component invocation is a relatively expensive operation, compared to a plain Java object method invocation, especially in container implementations that use Java reflection mechanisms extensively (which is a common practice nowadays). The CPU consumption of a service request depends on *how many* component invocations are involved in its execution and on the *types* of the invoked components. It is generally true that the invocation of a method on an entity EJB is more expensive, than on a session bean (partly because of the need to synchronize an EJB's state with the database), and that stateful session beans are more expensive than stateless ones.

RMI serialization. Early EJB container implementations used RMI for all inter-component communication, even for components residing within the same JVM. This approach imposes significant RMI serialization/deserialization overheads [26, 48]. With the introduction of EJB 2.0 *local interfaces*, it became possible to specify component *collocation*, which allows EJB containers to avoid using RMI for inter-component communication. To reduce the cost of marshalling, some application servers provide communication optimizations for components residing in the same JVM (even if they don't use EJB local interfaces), by using local object references instead of going through RMI.

Communication with the database. Accessing the database also entails serializing data back and forth from the database space to the JVM memory space. Inefficiently structured JDBC code can significantly limit application performance. The most prominent example of this situation is synchronization of entity beans with the database, which by default happens on every business method invoked on the entity bean [48]. A common misconception is that the problem is bandwidth, while the problem is the CPU overhead for writing and reading an object's data to/from the wire. Modern application servers provide facilities to limit unnecessary entity bean database synchronization, for example, by updating the state of the bean only before the method call, if the call is read-only. Some application servers also provide advanced mechanisms for caching data in entity beans.

Contention for exclusively-held server resources. Some of the server resources are shared among requests, while some are held exclusively by a request for the whole duration or a portion of it. Examples of the former include low-level OS resources, such as CPU and memory, while the latter are represented by such middleware resources as *server threads* and *database connections.* In the situation of server overload (static or transient), these resources become a source of request contention, with internal request queues building up. It is sometimes the case that the application performance is limited by such exclusively held "bottleneck" resources, even when there is enough CPU power to process more requests.

Transactions. It is well known that the transaction configuration of entity EJB containers, namely their *transaction commit options* (i.e., the server policies for lifecycle management of entity bean objects and their synchronization with the database), has significant impact on application server performance [22]. Transaction demarcation also influences the performance of Java EE applications, where longer transactions limit application scalability. This happens, because when the execution of a business method on an EJB is wrapped in a transaction, then, based on particular application configuration, the component may be blocked from other invocations. This means that other requests can't concurrently invoke a method on the same EJB component, which introduces a locking contention bottleneck, increasing client response times and limiting application scalability. More

28

fine-grained transaction demarcation, which however preserves application correctness, boosts application performance, especially when application logic involves sending and receiving asynchronous messages [75].

Application implementation method. The application implementation method has a significant impact on application performance [26]. Java EE applications with session beans perform as well as Java servlets-only applications and an order-of-magnitude better than most of the implementations based on entity beans. The fine-granularity access exposed by entity beans limits scalability, which however can be improved using session façade beans. For implementations using session façade beans, local communication cost is critically important, but EJB local interfaces (or application server optimizations substituting the use of the latter) improve performance by avoiding the RMI communication layers for local communications.

2.3 JBoss application server

To evaluate the cost and benefits of the server-side resource management mechanisms proposed in this work, we have implemented them in JBoss [68], an open source Java EE application server. JBoss is an extensible, reflective, and dynamically reconfigurable Java application server. In addition to including a set of components that implement the Java EE specification, JBoss is open-ended middleware in the sense that users can extend middleware services by dynamically deploying new service components into a running server. Throughout this work, if not stated otherwise, we use JBoss version 3.2.3, which is bundled with the HTTP/web server and Servlet/JSP container Jetty version 4.1.0 [69].

2.3.1 JBoss middleware architecture design

Modern industry-level Java EE application servers exhibit componentized architecture designs and usually are realized as a collection of independent, but related *middleware services*, each of which is dedicated to a particular aspect of application runtime support, e.g. transaction coordinator, naming service, security manager, etc. JBoss follows this approach. Its middleware architecture design is based on the Java Management Extensions (JMX) [117] specification. JMX defines an architecture, the design patterns, the APIs, and the services for management and monitoring of resources (applications, systems, or network devices). In JMX, to instrument a resource one has to associate one or more *management components* (*MBeans* in JMX) with the resource.

On top of JMX, JBoss introduces its own model for middleware components [81, 49], centered on the concept of a *service component*. The JBoss service component model extends and refines the JMX model to address some issues beyond the scope of JMX: service lifecycle, dependencies between services, deployment and redeployment of services, dynamic configuration and reconfiguration of services, and component packaging. Nearly all the application server functionality of JBoss is modularly provided by service components plugged into a JMX-based server spine, following the microkernel design principle. Service components implement every key feature of Java EE: naming service, transaction management, security service, EJB support, JMS messaging, and database connection pooling. They also implement important features not specified by Java EE, like clustering and fail-over. This architecture makes it easy to enhance the application server with the desired functionality, by implementing and deploying additional MBeans (service components). Moreover, MBeans in JBoss are *hot-deployable*.

2.3.2   JBoss EJB invocation model

As a part of the EJB invocation model, JBoss defines *client-side* and *server-side interceptors* [112, 49]. Interceptors act like *pluggable aspects*. When an EJB component method is invoked, the execution control first traverses the chain of client-side interceptors in the client JVM, then, upon reaching the server JVM, it goes through the chain of server-side interceptors (see Fig. 2.2). When the client obtains a reference to a remote EJB, it gets a *dynamic proxy* object, together with a set of client-side interceptors. One of the interesting consequences of this design is that client-side interceptors may execute arbitrary Java code in the client JVM, if this is not explicitly

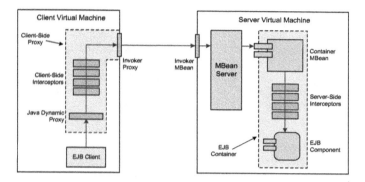

Figure 2.2: JBoss invocation model.

prevented by the Java security mechanisms. The JBoss modular remote invocation model also allows flexible choice of the *Invoker*, which is responsible for the communication mechanism between the client and server machines. The standard options in JBoss are JRMP (based on RMI — the default option), IIOP, HTTP, and SOAP [146] invokers.

The set of standard EJB client- and server-side interceptors can be extended and instantiated on a per-component basis. This functionality allows us to add, as we describe in Section 3.5.1, additional interceptors in order to gather request profiling information and to control the flow of request execution (e.g., to reject a method invocation).

2.4 Sample Java EE applications

To test the techniques proposed in this work, we have used three sample Java EE applications. One of these, an implementation of the TPC-W benchmark application, was developed by ourselves. The other two applications — Java Pet Store and RUBiS — were developed elsewhere.

2.4.1 TPC-W

TPC-W [133] is a transactional web e-Commerce benchmark, which emulates an on-line store that sells books. TPC-W specifies the application data structure and the functionality of the service, however it neither provides implementation, nor limits implementation to any specific technology. The TPC-W specification describes in detail the 14 web invocations that constitute the web site functionality, and defines how they change the application data stored in the database. Users can browse through a catalog of products, search for specific items and place them in a shopping cart. Upon indicating readiness to buy what is in the shopping cart, the application displays a bill detailing prices and quantities. Users can also create a permanent account with the on-line store, which includes billing and shipping information. Table 2.1 describes the most important service requests that make up a typical TPC-W user session.

We have developed our own implementation of the TPC-W benchmark, realized as a Java EE component-based application [132]. The implementation utilizes the *Session Façade* design pattern [85]. For each type of service request there is a separate servlet which, if necessary to generate the response HTML page, invokes business method(s) on associated session bean(s), that in turn access application shared data stored in the database through a set of fine-grained invocations to the related entity EJBs.

The TPC-W specification describes in detail the application data that should populate the database. The database population is defined by two parameters: NUM_ITEMS — the cardinality of the ITEM table, and NUM_EBS — the number of concurrent *Emulated Browsers (EB's)*, i.e., it is defined by the size of the store and size of the supported customer population. The size of the TPC-W database tables are fixed or depends linearly on the above two parameters. Application performance (i.e., the speed of processing database SQL queries) depends directly on the size of the database population.

Table 2.1: Main TPC-W service requests.

Request	Functionality
Home	Entry point to the application
Search	Performs search for specific items and presents them
New products	Presents items recently appeared in the store, for a specific category
Best Seller	Presents the list of items frequently purchased lately, for a specific category
Item Details	Presents the item details, including available quantity and price
Add To Cart	Adds item to the shopping cart, and displays its contents
Cart	Presents contents of the shopping cart
Register	Prompts user to authenticate or register itself
Buy Request	Authenticates or registers user, presents the updated view of the shopping cart, prompts user to submit address and credit cart information
Buy Confirm	Commits the order: records the order info in the database, decrements the available quantities for the items purchased, presents confirmation page

2.4.2 Java Pet Store

Java Pet Store [120] is a best-practices sample application from the Java Enterprise BluePrints program maintained by Sun Microsystems. It represents a typical e-Commerce application — an online store that sells pets (Table 2.2 describes service requests of the application). Java Pet Store aims at covering as much of the Java EE component platform as possible in a relatively small application. Its main focus is on design patterns and industry best practices that promote code and design reuse, extensibility, modularity, ease of maintenance, isolation of development tasks by skill sets, and decoupling of code-bases with differing rates of change. Therefore, Java Pet Store is a relatively heavy-weight application, compared to our TPC-W implementation and the RUBiS application described next.

The fundamental design pattern used in Java Pet Store is the *Model-*

33

Table 2.2: Java Pet Store service requests.

Request	Functionality
Main	Serves as an entry point to the application
Category	Displays list of products associated with a particular category
Product	Displays list of items associated with a particular product
Item	Displays details about an item, including description, price, and the quantity in stock
Search	Displays list of products, whose names match the specified search keyword(s)
Sign-in	Prompts user to enter user ID and password
Verify Sign-in	System authenticates submitted credentials
Shopping Cart	Upon the user adding an item to the shopping cart, the updated cart content is displayed
Checkout	User initiates checkout process
Place Order	User confirms the order
Billing and Shipping	User confirms billing and shipping information
Commit Order	User commits order; all necessary database updates happen here
Sign-out	User signs out

View-Controller (MVC) architecture [108], which decouples the application's data structure, business logic, data presentation, and user interaction. The *Model* represents the structure of the data in the application, as well as application-specific operations on that data. The *View* consists of objects that deal with presentation aspects of the application. The implementation of the View in Java Pet Store is completely contained in the Web tier, and is built on top of a reusable framework for web applications. The *Controller* translates user actions and inputs into method calls on the Model, and selects the appropriate View based on user preferences and Model state. Figure 2.3 shows the component relationships among the most accessed Java Pet Store components; and Table 2.3 describes the business function of the most important application EJBs.

34

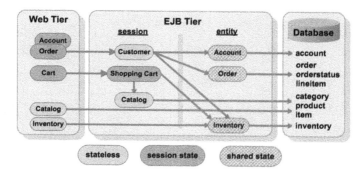

Figure 2.3: Java Pet Store component architecture.

2.4.3 RUBiS

RUBiS (Rice University Bidding System) [96, 131] is an auction site prototype modeled after the popular e-Commerce web portal eBay.com [42]. RUBiS implements the core functionality of an auction web site: selling, browsing and bidding on items. Visitors can search through a catalog of items divided into several categories and belonging to different geographical regions. They can bid on items of interest, as well as add comments for other users. Users may also choose to sell an item, registering it and specifying several parameters, such as action duration, and initial, reserve and buy-now prices. All non-browsing activities require creation of a permanent account with the web site and logging in. Table 2.4 describes the most important service requests of the RUBiS application.

RUBiS was originally developed at Rice University as part of a study investigating the combined effect of application implementation method, container design, and efficiency of communication layers on the performance scalability of Java EE applications [26]. Several implementations of the application were constructed, ranging from a servlets-only implementation, to one utilizing session and entity beans. We use the *Session Façade* implementation, where each servlet has reference(s) to dedicated stateless

Table 2.3: EJBs in Java Pet Store.

Name	Type	Description
Catalog	Stateless Session Bean	Serves as a façade to the product and inventory information
Product	Entity Bean	Keeps product-related information for each product line in the catalog
Item	Entity Bean	Keeps product-related information for each item in the catalog
Inventory	Entity Bean	Keeps availability information for each item in the catalog
ShoppingCart	Stateful Session Bean	Maintains list of items to be bought by customer
ShoppingClient-Controller	Stateful Session Bean	Manages the life cycle of business objects and processes events
SignOn	Entity Bean	Keeps userid/password information
Order	Entity Bean	Keeps order information
Account	Entity Bean	Keeps account information
Customer	Stateless Session Bean	Serves as a façade to Order and Account

session bean(s) only (almost always to just one such bean), which in turn access related entity beans. RUBiS does not keep per-client session state, so it neither keeps any (HTTP session) data in the web tier, nor does it use stateful session beans in the EJB tier. As a consequence of this design, there is no notion of a "logged in" user session in RUBiS, i.e., sessions where the user logs in and performs an arbitrary sequence of activities that do not require further authentication. User authentication is required before each essential non-browsing client activity and covers only one such activity.

2.5 Web workloads

Research studies investigating web user workloads can be divided into two groups. The work in the first group analyzes parameters of web workloads, by statistically processing web access logs, or using on-line profiling of

Table 2.4: Main RUBiS service requests.

Request	Functionality
Main	Static page; serves as an entry point to the application
Browse	Static page; displays several browsing options
All Categories	Displays the list of available categories
All Regions	Displays the list of regions
Region	Displays the list of available categories for a region
Category	Displays the list of available items in a category
Category and Region	Displays the list of available items in a category and a region
Item	Displays details about an item, such as current price and number of bids
Bids	Displays the list of bids on an item
User Info	Displays public information about a user, such as e-mail, current rating and the list of user comments
Put Bid Auth	Prompts bidder to enter User ID and password to put bid on an item
Put Bid Form	After verifying user credentials, system displays the bidding form
Store Bid	The bid is accepted and stored in the database
Put Comment Auth	Prompts user to authenticate him/herself, to proceed with writing a comment
Put Comment Form	After verifying user credentials, system displays the form for writing a comment
Store Comment	The comment is accepted and stored in the database

incoming user requests using instrumented servers. The results of these efforts are the set of broadly adopted assumptions or "laws" about statistical parameters and "invariants" of web user load. The work in the second group addresses the problems of web workload *simulation*, i.e., building adequate and realistic web workload *models*, which would be capable of producing streams of user requests, representative of real life user load.

2.5.1 Workload characterization

Request-based workload characterization

In the early days of the Internet, research concentrated on characterizing web workloads composed of individual requests to web pages, without considering the correlation between the requests coming from the same user. A number of studies [10, 13, 35, 100, 40, 23, 144] identified several characteristics, statistical properties, and invariants of these web workloads. Some of the widely used characterizations include: (1) 10% of all documents account for 90% of all requests and bytes transferred; (2) web page sizes follow a heavy-tailed *Pareto* distribution; (3) the web page inter-request times are independent and exponentially distributed, assuming a *Poisson* arrival process [73]; and (4) the popularity of documents served by information provider web sites follows *Zipf's Law* [23].

Session-based workload characterization

More recently, the Internet has changed from simply being a data repository and a communication infrastructure to becoming a medium for conducting business and selling services. This shift has resulted in changes in parameters of WWW traffic and the characteristics of web user workloads, with session-oriented interactions of users with Internet services becoming the norm.

The authors of [34] were among the first to acknowledge the changed nature of web user workloads. Since then several studies have characterized web workloads at the session level [89, 90, 11, 12, 87, 107] and have proven beneficial for research in the area of user-oriented management and optimization of Internet services, based on better understanding of service usage by clients. Following this path, the work in [76] first proposed a workload characterization for e-Commerce servers, where users followed typical sequences of URLs as they progressed towards the completion of sessions ("transactions"). This observation led to the notion of a *service access pattern*, a frequently executed scenario of service usage reflecting typical client behavior, which emerged in several studies [15, 26, 82]. Among several parameters of session-oriented web workloads we focus on the following two important characteristics: *new session arrivals* and *session inter-request times*.

It is generally believed that times between *new session arrivals* are well modeled by an exponential distribution, which corresponds to a Poisson arrival process and fits well into the framework of the classic Queueing Theory [73]. Session inter-request times is a more subtle issue. Work in [16, 35] reports that session inter-request times follow a Pareto distribution, while [107] points that it is best captured by a *log-normal* distribution. These studies analyze web access logs obtained from web servers of educational organizations. Studies which analyze request logs of e-Commerce web sites report that session inter-request times have either an exponential [34] or a Lognormal [12] distribution. One could ascribe the difference in reported session inter-request times to the nature of the service offered by a web site.

2.5.2 Workload simulation models

Utilizing synthetic web workloads is a common and widely adopted way to evaluate web server performance. Although not as realistic as using real web traces, this approach is more convenient for controlled exploration of a range of user behaviors. Several research efforts have pursued the goal of building adequate and realistic web workload models, which would be capable of producing streams of user requests representative of a real-life user load. These models are usually based on detailed analyses of real web access logs.

In [77] the authors propose the use of a sophisticated method of web trace generation, where user sessions consist of a controlled mix of actual session request sequences (*sessionlets*), taken from real web traces. The mix of sessionlets is adjusted to meet the target values of the attributes of the combined user load, such as session length distribution, request mix, etc. While this approach to web workload generation may produce realistic web access logs, its applicability is limited by the necessity to use real web traces, which are not always available in the public domain.

As a result, a dominant fraction of existing web workload models [89, 90, 25, 109, 45, 30], as well as the workload generators of web server performance benchmarks, such as TPC-W [133], use first or higher-order Markov chains to model session structures. The authors of the *Customer Behavior Model Graph (CBMG)* approach [89] were the first to introduce a first-order Markov chain to model user sessions. CBMG is a state transition graph, where states denote results of service requests (web pages), and transitions denote possible service invocations. Transitions in CBMG are governed by probabilities $p_{i,j}$ of moving from state i to state j ($\sum_j p_{i,j} = 1$). It was also shown that if one uses a mix of several CBMG session structures, then the resulting workload can approximate a given web access log as closely as desired, by appropriately choosing the model parameters (i.e., the number of CBMGs and their transition probabilities). The latter in turn can be obtained from the web access logs by using a clustering algorithm.

2.6 Performance of Internet services

High availability (i.e., ability to serve user requests) and responsiveness (i.e., adequate request response times) are two crucial service performance characteristics. Overloading a service immediately results in increased response times and request rejections, which leads to user dissatisfaction. On the other hand, ensuring the delivery of reasonable or prenegotiated quality of service (QoS) to users proves to be a nontrivial task, especially under high or varying user loads. The previous work addressing this problem can be roughly divided into three categories: (1) admission control and scheduling, (2) service differentiation, and (3) analytical modeling of Internet services.

2.6.1 Admission control and scheduling

Various forms of *admission control* have been used to prevent services from being overwhelmed in the presence of persistent or transient overload. Among these, Session-Based Admission Control (SBAC) [34] is suitable for session-oriented client loads. SBAC methods recognize that an overloaded service can experience a severe loss of throughput measured in completed (successful) sessions while still maintaining its throughput measured in requests per second. This happens because a request can be rejected anywhere in the session, even if the session has already had a lot of its requests served and is very close to completion. The SBAC methods works by admitting as many sessions as can be processed by the service, trying to make sure that if a client starts a session with the service, it will be successfully completed. The strategy is based on a self-tunable admission control function, which adjusts itself accordingly to variations in user load.

In recent years, several researchers have investigated the effects of request *scheduling* and *prioritization* on web server performance, for both web sites providing static content [33, 36, 103] and database-driven dynamic web sites [20, 45]. It has been shown that request response times and server throughput can be improved by employing such scheduling algorithms as Shortest Job First (SJF) [33, 36, 45] and Shortest Remaining Processing Time First [103]. Some of these studies used request scheduling algorithms combined with admission control policies [20, 21, 32, 45].

In web studies focusing on static content, the *cost* of servicing a job is usually approximated by the size of the downloaded file. For web sites serving dynamic content, it was noticed that request processing times depend primarily on the *request type* rather than on the parameters of the request [32, 45]. Our work shares the same observation, using fine-grained request profiling to determine first absolute and then relative request processing times for different request types. An analogous technique is used in [45].

A notable difference from the work in this book is that for the most part, the request scheduling studies above do not pursue the goal of increasing likelihood of session completion (even if they take into account the session-oriented nature of client workloads). An exception is the work of Chen et al. [30] on the Dynamic Weighted Fair Sharing request scheduling algorithm (DWFS), which, among other goals, tries to avoid processing of requests that belong to sessions that are likely to be aborted in the near future.

Several previous studies have also proposed admission control and request scheduling techniques that take into account application-specific information about the reward or profit brought to the Internet service by individual request types, and try to maximize this reward. In [148], a Profit Aware QoS policy (PAQoS) is developed, aimed at maximizing the web site's profit under SLA (service level agreement) constraints. The authors of [25] propose using queuing of requests based on their types, where a reward function corresponding to the service provider's objective is maximized using techniques for nonlinear optimization. In [109], the authors propose a combined LIFO-Priority scheme for overload control of a retail e-Commerce web site, where all service requests are divided among browser and (in their terminology) *revenue-generating transaction* requests (i.e., reward-bringing requests in our terminology). LIFO scheduling is applied to the browser requests, while the revenue-generating requests are given the highest priority.

There are conceptual differences between these studies and the approach proposed in this book. In [148, 25, 109], the authors assume that reward is brought by individual requests, rather than by completion of the whole session. In [148, 25], they also assume a Generalized Processor Sharing (GPS) [149] model for request execution, rather than a model of prioritized scheduling of requests to *exclusively-held* resources, such as server threads and DB connections (Section 3.3.1). In our opinion, the latter model is a closer match to existing web application server architectures.

2.6.2 Service differentiation

Policies for *quality differentiation* among multiple classes of service have been investigated in recent literature. In the simplest case, the service is differentiated between two classes of clients, *premium* and *basic*, such that premium clients receive better service than basic clients in case of overload. The authors of [44] proposed and evaluated policies that impose restrictions on the amount of server resources (such as threads) available to basic clients. In [9, 1] admission control and scheduling algorithms were enhanced with QoS-aware client differentiation mechanisms, to provide premium clients with better QoS, in the context of web content hosting and multimedia servers, respectively.

The work in [83, 2] was innovative in that it proposed using *feedback-control* theory and methodology to design an adaptive connection scheduler and process reallocation strategies to provide relative request delay guarantees for different service classes, in the context of HTTP servers providing static web content. The authors of [29] proposed a tiered system for serving differentiated content, which transparently routes user queries to heterogeneous web server back ends, based on explicit user requirements for latency and quality of data.

A way to control QoS delivered to users and to efficiently manage server resources is through *service level agreements* (SLA), also called *resource sharing agreements*. SLA is a contract between a service user group and the service provider, establishing the parameters of and limiting service usage by the user group. This way the service provider can estimate the level of service usage and resource consumption. Common to all service differentiation schemes is the consideration that the quality of service received by a user is determined upfront by his association with a client group or by his service membership status.

2.6.3 Analytical modeling of Internet services

Analytical modeling of the behavior of Internet applications is beneficial for the following reasons: (1) *capacity provisioning* [88], which allows one to determine how much capacity is needed for an application to allow it to service the specified workload; (2) *performance prediction*, which enables the response time of the application to be determined for a given workload and a given hardware and software configuration; (3) *application configuration*, which enables various configuration parameters of the application to be determined for a certain performance goal; and (4) *bottleneck identification and tuning*, which enables system bottlenecks to be identified for purposes of performance tuning.

The vast majority of analytical models of Internet applications utilize the apparatus of Queueing Theory [73], while some use Markov chains [86] and control-theoretical approaches [83, 2]. Modeling of single-tier Internet applications, of which HTTP servers are the most common example, has been studied extensively [110, 86, 41, 136]. Most of these studies also assume static web content. However, modern data-centric applications serve dynamic web content and tend to utilize multi-tier architectures

43

(Section 2.2.1). Several recent efforts have focused on the modeling of multi-tier applications [71, 135]. However, many of these efforts either make simplifying assumptions or are based on simple extensions of single-tier models. A number of papers have taken the approach of modeling only the most constrained or the most bottlenecked tier of the application. For instance, [139] considers the problem of provisioning servers for only the middle (EJB) tier. Other efforts have modeled the entire multi-tier application using a single queue [113]. While these efforts have made good progress, analytical modeling of Internet applications remains a hard problem, because of complex structural and behavioral properties of these applications.

2.7 Transaction processing and concurrency control techniques

The field of *transaction processing* [58, 19] is concerned with the correctness of concurrent and distributed execution of programs accessing shared data, which relates to our problem of providing web sessions with data integrity guarantees (Section 1.2.3). Web sessions of Internet services where the service provider wants to limit the degree of session data inconsistency may be viewed as long-running open-ended "transactions" with specific data consistency constraints.

2.7.1 Classical concurrency control techniques

In the classical model of transaction processing, correct execution of transactions assumes that the following four properties (*ACID* properties) are satisfied:

- **Atomicity**: Either all of the tasks of a transaction are performed or none of them are. A transaction that executes successfully is called a *committed* transaction, while a transaction that can not be executed to preserve ACID properties is *aborted*, so that all its effects are *undone* and are not visible at any moment to other transactions/clients.

- **Consistency**: Transaction preserves the internal consistency of the database (of course, if the submitted operations themselves do not violate database consistency). This property is somewhat outdated and arises from the earlier formal models of transaction execution, which was thought of as moving the database from one consistent state to another. The consistency property is actually implied by the existence of the other three properties and is being cited mainly due to historical reasons.

- **Isolation**: A transaction executes as if it is running alone. The technical definition of isolation is *serializability*. The execution of a set of transactions (i.e., the order of execution of transactions' operations) is said to be serializable if it is equivalent to some serial execution (i.e., one after another — in a sequence). This guarantees transaction isolation.

- **Durability**: Transaction results will not be lost in a failure. That is, if a transaction commits and the transaction client is notified of its success, its results are durably stored in the database.

Clients explicitly specify transaction boundaries and interact with *Transaction Processing Monitors*, which (1) receive transaction operations from clients; (2) reorder, block, and buffer these operations, if necessary to avoid conflicts and to satisfy transaction isolation properties; (3) schedule operations for actual execution; and (4) commit or abort transactions. The process of ensuring correct execution of transactions is called *concurrency control* and is achieved by various concurrency control techniques. The most famous and the most used technique is *Two-Phase Locking (2PL)*. The idea of this technique is to *lock* a data item from concurrent operations of other transactions, for the duration of the transaction accessing the data item. This and related locking techniques are sometimes called *pessimistic*, because they conservatively lock data items, blocking execution of operations of concurrent transactions, until the lock is released.

45

2.7.2 Web sessions with data integrity constraints

Before we discuss concurrency control techniques most related to our work let us summarize the properties of web sessions and show how concurrent web sessions with data integrity constraints (Section 1.2.3) differ from existing transaction models.

- Web sessions do not have well defined boundaries. They are interactive, open-ended, user-driven, often long-running activities. A session (accurately speaking, its rendering in the web server) ends only by timeout.

- ACID properties: session data integrity constraints relate to the "C" and "I" aspects of the ACID properties. We are neither concerned with atomicity, nor do we care about durability, because it is the responsibility of the underlying middleware to persistently store the results of executed requests.

- Locking concurrency control techniques assume that an operation can be arbitrary blocked (e.g., buffered, waiting for a lock) before being executed. In web sessions, inter-request times are much higher than request execution times. Therefore, requests waiting for shared resources can not be blocked forever, as clients, especially human ones, are typically willing to tolerate only small response delays.

- It is highly undesirable to *rollback* a web session, by "undoing" its effects. It is possible to "compensate" the results of the aborted web session (for example, by sending an e-mail to the client). However, such behavior of the service will most probably bring user dissatisfaction.

- Some transaction models allow automatic reexecution of aborted transactions, or single transaction operations, by Transaction Processing Monitors on behalf of clients. This can not be done in the context of interactive real-time client-service communication models inherent to web sessions.

2.7.3 Advanced transaction models and concurrency control techniques

The use of transaction models in non-traditional applications has become widespread and it has been found that classical transactions have limited applicability for these applications. Among numerous proposed advanced transaction models [67, 17], there are several research efforts that are relevant to our work.

Optimistic concurrency control techniques. Locking (pessimistic) concurrency control techniques present one end of the concurrency control spectrum. At the other end of the spectrum lie *optimistic* approaches to concurrency control [78]. The main idea of these techniques is that the operations are scheduled as they are received by the Transaction Monitor. When a transaction wants to commit it is *validated* against concurrent active transactions, to check that the resulted schedule of transaction operations is serializable (i.e., no conflicts have happened). There are two main flavors of validation: *backward* validation checks that the committing transaction was not invalidated by other transactions, and if so — aborts the committing transaction; while *forward* validation always commits the transaction and aborts concurrent transactions that are invalidated by this commit. It has been acknowledged that pessimistic approaches are more suitable for transaction mixes with a high rate of conflicts, while optimistic ones are better for lower rates of conflicts, for example for query dominated systems.

Mixed concurrency control techniques. While optimistic and pessimistic concurrency control techniques represent two extremes, several studies have proposed so-called *mixed* or *hybrid* concurrency control strategies, which combine the elements of both optimistic and pessimistic approaches. Earlier work in this direction [64] proposed mixed concurrency control schemes where a user directly specifies which pairs of conflicting operations should be covered by optimistic and pessimistic concurrency control techniques. In [99], the authors explore a hybrid technique that automatically provides locking for high conflict data items and optimistic access for the rest. The system uses an LRU data structure called the *lock buffer* for data items covered by the pessimistic (locking) concurrency control technique. If an item gets evicted from the lock buffer, all transactions accessing this item "become" optimistic with respect to the evicted data item.

Semantic-based concurrency control. Several researchers have proposed using semantic knowledge of the system to determine logical correctness of transaction execution, instead of mandating a serializable schedule. The work on semantics-based concurrency control can be classified into two major categories. In the first category [63, 64, 141, 14] the authors exploit the *semantics of operations* to increase concurrency. Instead of using operations such as read and write, the authors propose using higher-level operations to access data objects. Commutativity of these operations is used to determine conflicts between transactions, resulting in more concurrency. The work in the second category [3, 47, 55] exploits *semantics of transactions* to increase concurrency, by decomposing transactions into steps and developing semantics-based correctness criteria for transaction execution.

Relaxed consistency. Another approach to increase concurrency is to *relax isolation* or *consistency* properties of transaction execution [145, 3, 39, 147]. The main idea of these techniques is that transactions are allowed to conflict with each other, by accessing shared data items, but only to a certain degree. The *degree of conflict* between transactions can be measured across two dimensions. The first dimension reflects the *numerical error* — e.g., how can an item's value change from its initial value (when the item was first accessed by the transaction). One could define *relative* or *absolute* tolerable degrees of discrepancy. The second dimension reflects the *order error* — how many conflicting operations of other transactions can be executed. Relaxed consistency is best combined with optimistic concurrency approaches, when the Transaction Manager checks during the validation phase that the transaction's relaxed consistency requirements are not violated. Formal models of relaxed consistency, such as *epsilon serializability (ESR)* [101] have also been developed.

48

Long-running transactions. There are several proposals addressing transactional needs of *long-running* activities and business processes [57, 56, 37, 105, 18]. Acknowledging the fact that conventional transaction models (those viewing transaction as an indivisible process) can not be used for long-running activities, these studies focus mainly on the aspects of *dividing* long-running activities into *sub-transactions*, and on related problems, such as the sharing of partially committed data, multi-stage execution, recovery and compensation, etc. Web sessions share a commonality with these transaction models in that they also can be viewed as long-running activities. However, the assumptions of these models are that long-running transactions, as classical ones, are demarcated and divided by programmers. Web sessions don't have well defined boundaries and are not divided into sub-transactions.

Conversational and cooperative transactions. In some of their properties, web sessions resemble advanced transaction models, such as *conversational transactions* [142] and *cooperative transactions* [94, 70]. Conversational transactions are "chopped" into a chain of smaller transactions, each of which corresponds to receiving a message and sending a reply. Previous work on conversational transactions has primarily focused on providing mechanisms to durably store and efficiently recover the conversation context, rather than dealing with data conflicts; in the web sessions context, the former problem admits simple solutions such as the use of HTTP cookies (although these are not 100% failure resilient [142]), while the latter issue has not received as much attention. Cooperative transactions are used in systems like CAD (Computer Aided Design), where several concurrent users perform different tasks with the shared data, and are interested in sharing of (partial) results with each other, retaining some of the transactional properties of the execution process. Like web sessions, cooperative transactions are also viewed as long-running, open-ended activities with a user-defined notion of correctness of execution. However, cooperative transactions delegate much of the control to the clients, who explicitly manage shared resources and transaction isolation.

2.7.4 Analytical modeling of transactions

Analytical modeling of concurrency control mechanisms is a well studied problem [127, 4, 129, 130]. However, while working on this book, we were unable to find a model for concurrency control that would specifically cover the case of web sessions with data integrity constraints. As rightfully pointed out in [4], "nearly every study is based on its own unique set of assumptions regarding database system resources, transaction behavior, and other such issues." Most previous models have focused on modeling classical database transactions which enforce strict consistency. However our concurrency control algorithms for web sessions with data integrity constraints (see Section 6.2.2) have some notable differences from their classical counterparts. In conventional database transactions, it is acknowledged that *pessimistic* (locking) concurrency control approaches are more suitable for higher rates of conflicts, while *optimistic* ones work well for lower conflict rates [4]. As we will see, in the web sessions case, the situation is opposite. This performance difference observed in preliminary simulations, also steered us to creation of our own analytical models (Section 6.3). We believe that the difference between the classical locking and our locking concurrency control mechanisms (Section 6.2.2) is the main reason why optimistic and locking approaches have the opposite behavior in classical transactions and in the case of web sessions. Interestingly, there are some similarities between our results and the results of previous studies in the area of *real-time* database transactions [62, 134]. Such transactions have associated *completion deadlines* that they have to meet in order to be successful. Real-time database transactions share a commonality with web sessions in that optimistic approaches often outperform the locking ones.

2.8 Content and service distribution

A noticeable trend in the design and utilization of Internet services is to bring application data and data processing *closer to the clients*. This is being done in order to cope, on the network level, with the unpredictable nature of Internet traffic, especially in wide-area environments, and, on the application level, with high-volume, widely varying client workloads. Examples of this approach vary from old-fashioned web caching of static content to distribution of services realized as component-based applications.

2.8.1 Web caching and Content Distribution Networks

Web caching

The most common approach to efficient web content delivery is the use of web caching to improve the scalability of the web. Caches leverage the well known principle of reference locality. There are two flavors of locality: *temporal* and *spatial*. Temporal locality means that some pieces of data (web pages, in case of web caching) are accessed more frequently in a time period than others. Spatial locality means that requests for certain web pages are likely to occur together.

To improve caching effectiveness, several projects have proposed cooperative web caching [28, 46], which aims at establishing interactions among several caching peers. Although the cache hit rate of cooperative web caching increases only to a certain level, corresponding to a moderate population size [144], highly-scalable cooperative systems can still increase the total system throughput by reducing server-side load. With the growing interest in peer-to-peer systems, several projects have proposed using peer-to-peer systems for web caching [111, 106], although such systems only benefit participating clients and thus require widespread adoption to reduce server load.

Content Distribution Networks

Content Distribution Networks (CDN) were introduced as a natural evolution of existing web caching strategies, with the goal of further improving web scalability, reliability, and web-page response times for users. CDN is a system of computer nodes networked together across the Internet that cooperate in some fashion to deliver content to end users, by transparently moving content behind the scenes to optimize the delivery process. Many traditional CDNs focus on serving relatively static content from existing distribution infrastructures of participating service providers. Since the first Content Distribution Networks appeared nearly a decade ago, this field has rapidly grown into a successful segment of the Internet marketplace. Several commercial and academic CDNs are available nowadays.

Akamai [6] is the most successful commercial content delivery service. It operates thousands of dedicated servers located at network provider data centers around the world. Akamai distributes copies of its clients' content to these servers, and then, uses DNS redirection to reroute user requests to the clusters of machines closest to the user. Akamai and other commercial CDNs built on the same principles require the deployment of large numbers of highly provisioned servers, and typically result in very good performance (both latency and throughput) for customers.

A different approach is employed by the Coral CDN [51]. Coral is a decentralized, self-organizing, web-content distribution network that builds upon the ideas of peer-to-peer systems. It states the goal of allowing a user to run a web site that offers high performance and meets huge demand virtually without any distribution costs. Coral works by leveraging the aggregate bandwidth of volunteer sites running the Coral software to absorb and dissipate most of the traffic for web sites using the system. In doing so, Coral replicates content in proportion to the content's popularity, regardless of the publisher's resources — in effect democratizing content publication. However, Coral offers less aggregate storage capacity than commercial CDNs and, as a peer-to-peer system, requires wide adoption of the system to bring substantial performance benefits to its users.

2.8.2 Distribution of dynamic content

The success in distributing static web content is undermined by the increasingly large share of dynamic and personalized content in the overall volume of the content served on the web. Such content is dynamically generated at the original service provider web site in response to the request parameters, and therefore can not be immediately cached.

Caching of dynamic content

Despite the dynamically generated and personalized nature of web content, a relatively large amount of such content can in fact be shared. For example, certain web pages, although dynamically generated, present the same information to all users; a large portion of personalized web pages contain fragments identical for all web pages of the same type. This important observation makes it possible to reduce the load on the main service provider web site, by caching *parts* of the content at the *edge servers*.

Commercial systems such as Akamai's EdgeSuite [7] and IBM's WebSphere [65] utilize the following underlying idea: they distinguish between *content generation* (which is performed on the main service web site) and *content assembly* (which can be performed on the edge servers). These products rely on the Edge Side Includes (ESI) [43] standard specification, which includes a simple markup language used to define web page fragments and allows the dynamic assembly of these fragments into complete web pages at the edge servers. Dynamic web page assembly improves web site performance by caching the frequently reused and shared web page fragments at the edge of the Internet.

Several other research efforts have addressed the importance of caching dynamic content to improve system performance and scalability, even if such caching is performed in a Local Area Network (LAN) setting. The authors of [27] developed an approach for caching dynamic web data that became a critical component of the 1998 Olympic Winter Games web site. In the related study [38], *database query caching* was used to improve performance of the IBM's WebSphere application server [65]. The proposed techniques significantly reduced the number of queries to remote databases. A key problem faced was how to keep the cache valid after database updates. This was solved using Data Update Propagation (DUP) mechanism, which employed an update strategy that considered the values of database updates in order to perform intelligent cache invalidations.

Replication of application logic and data

A natural extension of content assembly at the edge servers is the idea of moving (or replicating) a part of *application business logic* to the edge servers. Now not only content assembly, but also content generation can be performed at the servers located closer to the clients. However, in data-centric applications that dominate modern Internet services, the business logic that processes user requests requires frequent accesses of shared data-sources. A key challenge in systems with distributed application logic is data replication and consistency so that application modules located at the edge servers can manipulate shared data without incurring the availability and performance penalties of accessing the centralized database. Therefore the question of moving application logic closer to clients is in great part conditioned on the question of efficiently ensuring consistency of replicated data.

The performance of a data replication algorithm is greatly affected by *client behavior*, i.e. by the nature of user request mix. Although it is impossible to simultaneously provide optimal consistency, availability, and performance for general-case wide-area network replication, it is possible to provide nearly optimal behavior for specific objects by taking advantage of a given application's workload characteristics.

The authors of [54] propose an object-based edge server architecture with a consistency model that takes advantage of *service access patterns* typical for e-Commerce retail applications. They design data consistency models for each individual distributed object by using the corresponding application-specific semantics. For example, the *Catalog* object is the abstraction of one-to-many updates, it accepts writes at one place and propagates changes to multiple locations for subsequent reads; the abstraction of the *Order* object is that of many-to-one updates, it gathers writes at various locations and forwards them to a single place for reading. High availability and efficiency of these application-specific distributed objects is achieved by slightly relaxing data consistency. In this regard, this work builds upon the ideas developed in the Bayou [98] and TACT [147] systems, which have explored the space of relaxed consistency models for state replication in wide-area systems. Bayou [98] proposes an anti-entropy protocol for flexible update propagation between weakly consistent storage replicas, and TACT [147] investigates tradeoffs between consistency, performance and availability of replicated services.

2.8.3 Distribution of component-based applications

Component-based applications, at a first glance, appear to be immediate candidates for distribution and replication in attempt to bring service closer to the clients. First, application components represent an indivisible unit of application logic, responsible for a particular service function, with well defined communication and deployment requirements. Second, most component frameworks offer mechanisms to enable distributed deployment of components, therefore application distribution would require only minimal changes to the application, mostly dealing with the application configuration parameters.

Though nominally suitable for distribution, applications utilizing commercial component models (such as Java EE [121] and CORBA [95]) are typically deployed and replicated only in a centralized fashion in high-performance local area networks. The replication of application components in current-day enterprise component-based systems is primarily performed in a local scale for failover and performance purposes [84, 79]. The component application servers involved in the replication are usually tightly clustered together, and low-level LAN-specific mechanisms such as IP broadcast, are used to synchronize among the replicas. Such tightly-coupled approaches do not scale to distributed environments, which require scalable and efficient mechanisms for inter-component synchronization.

Researchers have been reluctant to propose commercial component frameworks for edge service distribution. Inter-component communication and rigid specification-imposed limitations on the component lifecycle and management seem to be the key factor limiting the usability of these frameworks for the application distribution purposes. The authors of [80] have examined an edge server architecture in which a centralized database is shared among a number of edge servers that maintain cached copies of transactionally-consistent EJBs (Section 2.2). The results of this study have shown that such edge server architecture increases request latencies,

55

which is attributed to the needs of EJB synchronization with the centralized database. However, it decreases the consumed network bandwidth and increases request throughput by offloading some of the processing from the main server to the edge servers.

In the research arena, several component frameworks have been proposed to build scalable, flexible, and efficient distributed applications: Globus Grid [50], CANS [52], Ninja [59], and PSF [66] are representative examples. Typical applications deployed on these frameworks include collaborative visualization of large scientific datasets, computational intensive scientific applications, web-based mailing systems, applications serving media content, such as video conferencing and remote video, etc. However, other applications such as enterprise services and B2B partnerships are not prevented from being able to operate in such environments. These component frameworks concentrate on such issues as QoS-aware application adaptation in dynamically changing heterogeneous environments, providing security guarantees for applications deployed across multiple administrative domains, and maintaining data consistency across component replicas. The latter issue relates these research efforts to the problem of efficient edge replication of data-centric Internet services.

Chapter 3

Service Access Attributes

Information about service usage by clients can be exposed at different levels — from high-level structure of incoming request flow, to low level information about resource consumption and data access patterns of different request types. Some of this information can be automatically obtained by request profiling, some can be obtained by statically analyzing the application structure, while some needs to be specified by the service provider. In this book, we identify four related groups of *service access attributes*, that correspond to different levels of service usage information. The relationship between different service access attributes, which are described in detail below, is schematically shown in Fig. 3.1, which is taken from Section 1.2 and reproduced here for convenience.

3.1   Request flow

This service access attribute provides the high-level information about the requests that are being invoked against the service. The information about an individual service request is limited to its *type, session (client) identity*, and (optionally) the time of its arrival.

Request type corresponds to the functionality of a request. Typical component-based web applications follow a principle where separate servlets are reserved for processing requests of different functionality. Determining the servlet to use for processing of a request is usually done based

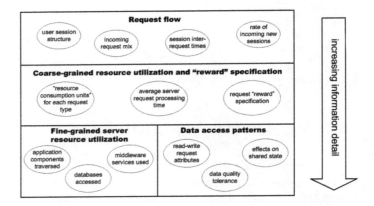

Figure 3.1: Four groups of service access attributes.

on the request's URL pattern, hence the type of a request can typically be determined by its URL. For example, in the TPC-W application, HTTP request

```
http://host_name/tpcw/item?id=57
```

would request a detailed description of the item with id 57, while HTTP request

```
http://host_name/tpcw/cart
```

would request the contents of the shopping cart. A request's URL would typically also contain request's parameters. In the above example of the Item Details request, the id of the item (57 in this case) is encoded in the request's URL. Thus, the organization of HTTP requests makes it possible to infer a request's type and its parameters at the earliest stage of request execution — request preprocessing at the web tier, enabling collection of request flow information through real-time profiling of incoming user requests.

The most common mechanism to encode session identity in HTTP requests is through the use of *HTTP cookies*. Another approach to do so is by *encoding* the session identity in the requested URL. In both cases (and in their variations) session management is performed automatically by the HTTP/web server, which keeps information about currently active web sessions and transfers the cookie or URL encoding information into internal programmatic representation of web sessions, used by application programmers.

Service usage information specified in the request flow service access attribute may come in different forms. For example, it may state the rate and the arrival pattern of the requests of certain types as they are received by the server. It may describe the (typical) structure(s) of incoming user sessions. Request flow information may contain various timing parameters, such as session inter-request times, or the rate of incoming new sessions. Models capturing the structure of request flow can be used to reproduce and simulate user activities, therefore the problem of representation of request flow information is tightly coupled with the problem of web workload generation.

3.1.1 Web session structure

A user session consists of a sequence of service requests, issued by a single user. These requests do not go in arbitrary order, because they adhere to the application logic of the service. In the realm of web-based services, the set of service requests that a user can make consists of the *HTML links* presented on the web page that was last displayed to the user, that is, it depends on the result of the previous request. Therefore generally, session structure can be captured by a *state transition diagram*, where states denote results of service requests (web pages), and arrows (transitions) denote possible service invocations. Note that this model does not capture different client behavior, such as manually typing a URL in the address bar of the browser, because generally, service providers discourage such user behavior and often even make it impossible, populating web links with hidden URL parameters and dynamically generated keys.

The set of possible transitions from a given state may depend on (1) the previous requests that user made in the session, i.e., on the *session state*, and (2) on the application *shared state*. The first category is exemplified by events such as user sign-in/sign-out (if the user is signed in, there will be an HTML link for signing out, and vice versa), or the contents of the shopping cart (e.g., if the shopping cart is empty, the there will be no HTML link to start the checkout process). The second category is exemplified by the cases such as an item being out of stock — there would normally be no link allowing addition of the item into the shopping cart.

3.1.2 Web session structure modeling — CBMG model

Whereas state transition diagrams producing possible web session structures can be arbitrarily complex, in most cases these diagrams have quite simple organization, or can be considerably simplified by only accounting for state transitions (and so — certain session structures) that represent *typical* user behavior for a given Internet service. For example, session structures can often be represented by *graphs*, where the set of possible state transitions (possible service requests) depends only on the current state (previous request).

In this work, we follow the trend to model web session structures by state transition diagrams (see also Section 2.5.1) and adopt the *Customer Behavior Model Graph* [89] approach to model user sessions. As proposed originally, Customer Behavior Model Graph (CBMG) is a plain state transition graph, where the set of possible transitions (service requests) does not depend on the implicit application (session or shared) state. In the CBMG model, state transitions are governed by transition probabilities $p_{i,j}$ of moving from state i to state j ($\sum_{j=1}^{N} p_{i,j} = 1$, where N is the number of states in the CBMG). In our model we also allow a *finite* number of *finite-domain attributes* for each state of the CBMG. These attributes can be used to represent session state, i.e., session events like signing-in and signing-out of an e-Commerce Web site, or the number of items put into the shopping cart, for an on-line store. The set of possible transitions and probabilities can in turn depend on the values of these attributes. Since the set of attributes and their values is finite, each extended CBMG may be reduced to an equivalent CBMG, by duplicating states for each possible combination of attribute

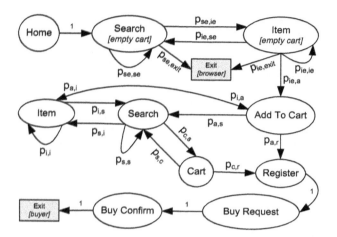

Figure 3.2: CBMG of a sample TPC-W buyer session.

values.

Fig.3.2 shows the CBMG of a sample *buyer* session for the TPC-W application (Section 2.4.1), which we will be frequently using in this book. This CBMG produces simplified user session structures, which use only a subset of the available TPC-W request types, but are rich enough to include essential application activities and represent requests with a wide range of functional and execution complexity. Each session modeled by this CBMG starts with the Home request, and may end either after several Search and Item Details (Item in short) requests (we refer to such sessions as *browser* sessions), or after putting one or more items in the shopping cart and completing the purchase (*buyer* session). Note that, for simplicity, we do not differentiate between the Search, New Products, and Best Sellers requests (see Section 2.4.1) and they are represented as one state. In the TPC-W web workloads using the presented CBMG we will be actually using the TPC-W Best Sellers request as the CBMG request of type *Search*. We have

61

one (boolean-valued) CBMG *state attribute* for the Search and Item states, which denotes the presence of items in the shopping cart, to model the assumption that once a user puts an item into the shopping cart, he never abandons the session and eventually commits the order. This assumption is introduced in order to stress essential buyer activities in this sample session scenario.

CBMG model can be augmented with additional information specifying parameters of the requests constituting a session. For example, in the TPC-W buyer CBMG presented above, each Item request carries an additional parameter — the `itemId` of the item to be displayed. If not stated otherwise, we assume that there are S items in the store, and that the i-th item is picked with probability p_i^{item}. The Add To Cart request chooses the same item that was picked in the preceding Item request, and it puts it in the shopping cart with quantity 1.

Timing parameters

Request flow information is often augmented with various timing parameters describing arrival patterns of service requests. In a session-oriented request flow specification, *session inter-request times* and *arrival patterns* of new sessions are the most commonly used timing parameters. It is usually assumed that session inter-request time is a random variable with a certain distribution, and its mean value T_{ir} (i.e., average session inter-request time) is one of the timing parameters of interest. For the arrivals of new user sessions, whatever this process looks like, we are interested in the average rate of incoming new sessions — λ, which reflects the intensity of the user load.

3.1.3   Request flow properties

Different service management problems addressed in this book are sensitive to different aspects of the request flow information. Below we list the request flow properties that we will be looking at in this work.

- RATE — overall request rate; RATE_i — rate of requests of a particular type i.

- V_i — average number of visits to state i (requests of type i) in a session.

- Breakdown of requests by their type: R_i — percentage of requests of type i.

- L_{av} — average session length (in requests).

- Timing parameters: T_{ir} — average session inter-request time, λ — rate of incoming new sessions.

- Specific properties of request sequences of web sessions, e.g., the relative occurrence and placement of certain requests in a session.

3.1.4 Request flow modeling (web workload generation)

There are two major approaches in modeling request flow — *request-oriented* and *session-oriented*. In this book, we will use both of them. Our approaches for doing so are described below.

Request-oriented workload specification

This workload is used in situations, where the session identity of requests is not relevant to the problem being examined. For generating this workload, we directly specify the values of RATE_i — rates of requests of different types. For each request type i, the flow of requests of that type is modeled as a Poisson process [73] with parameter RATE_i.

Session-oriented workload specification

This web workload consists of K CBMGs: $\mathrm{CBMG}_1, \mathrm{CBMG}_2, \ldots, \mathrm{CBMG}_K$. The probability of a session having the structure of CBMG_k is p_k, $\sum_{k=1}^{K} p_k = 1$. For a session of structure CBMG_k, the probabilities of state transitions are denoted $p_{i,j}^k$.

Following the discussion in Sections 2.5.1 and 2.5.2, we model session inter-request (user think) times as either exponentially ($\mathrm{Exp}(\mu)$) or log-normally ($\mathrm{Ln}(\mu, \sigma)$) distributed. In cases where the effects of having

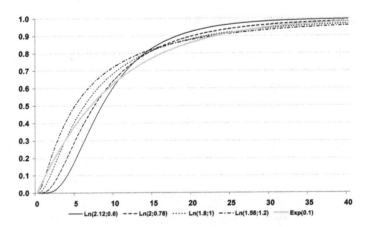

Figure 3.3: CDF of the exponential and four log-normal distributions, all having mean value 10.

different distributions of session inter-request times need to be compared, we use these distributions with the parameters chosen so that their mean values match ($E[\text{Exp}(\mu) = 1/\mu]$; $E[\text{Ln}(\mu;\sigma)] = e^{\mu+\sigma^2/2}$). To give the reader a feeling of how the two distributions differ, we show in Fig. 3.3, Cumulative Distribution Functions (CDF) of five distributions — Exp(0.1), Ln(2.12;0.6), Ln(2.12;0.6), Ln(1.8;1), and Ln(1.58;1.2) — all having mean value 10.

When not stated otherwise, the flow of incoming new sessions is modeled as a Poisson process with arrival rate λ. The Poisson process produces a relatively smooth sequence of events, and fails to model inherently bursty and self-similar traffic typically observed at web sites [140]. To better model the latter, we also use the B-model [140], which has been shown to produce synthetic traces with burstiness matching that of real web traffic. We use this model to produce load with different *degrees of burstiness* (determined by the b-parameter of the B-model), and do it in a way to only imitate local (short-lived) burstiness to avoid substantial shifting of mas-

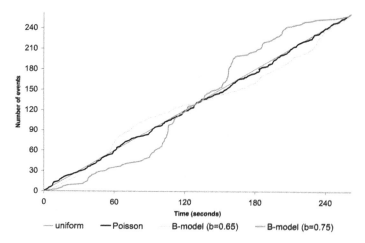

Figure 3.4: Event arrival patterns for the three processes: Poisson ($\lambda = 1$) and B-model ($b = 0.65$ and $b = 0.75$).

sive event clusters to short time intervals. Specifically, we model two types of bursty load, one with $b = 0.65$ and another with $b = 0.75$,[1] and refer to these as "low-bursty" and "high-bursty" load respectively. In contrast with these two methods, we refer to the Poisson arrival model as "smooth." Fig. 3.4 shows the event arrival patterns for a Poisson process ($\lambda = 1$), and for the two B-model processes ($b = 0.65$ and $b = 0.75$) with the same average event arrival rate (1 event/s). This graph helps to visually assess the degree of event arrival burstiness produced by different models.

The request flow parameters that we are looking at in this work (Section 3.1.3) can be extracted from the parameters of the CBMG-based session-oriented web workload. The values of V_i, the average number of visits to state i, can be obtained by solving the following system of linear equations

---

[1] In the original B-model study [140], the authors analyzed real web traces and inferred that the b-parameter for those traces ranged from 0.6 to 0.8, so we felt that values 0.65 and 0.75 would be reasonably representative.

(this apparatus was originally developed in [89]):

$$\begin{cases} V_1 & = & 1 \\ V_i & = & \sum_{k=1}^{N} V_k \cdot p_{k,i} \quad \text{for all } i = 2, \ldots, N \end{cases} \tag{3.1}$$

where V_1 is the entry state (e.g., the Home request in the CBMG in Fig. 3.2). The average session length is given by the equation

$$L_{\text{av}} = \sum_{i=1}^{N} V_i, \tag{3.2}$$

and the breakdown of requests by their type is given by

$$R_i = \frac{V_i}{L} \tag{3.3}$$

Finally, the overall request rate and request rates for specific request types are given by

$$\begin{aligned} \text{RATE} & = & \lambda \cdot L \\ \text{RATE}_i & = & \lambda \cdot V_i \quad \text{for } i = 1, \ldots, N \end{aligned} \tag{3.4}$$

In case the user load consists of several CBMGs, equations (3.1) – (3.4) are generalized in a straightforward manner using the probabilities associated with different CBMGs as a weighting factor.

3.2 Coarse-grained resource utilization and "reward"

This service access attribute contains information about the high-level "cost" of execution of requests of different types and the "profit" ("reward") that requests of different types bring to the service provider.

3.2.1 Coarse-grained request resource utilization

Requests of different types may exhibit different execution complexity and show different server resource consumption, because they tend to utilize different sets of application components and middleware services. Some requests, for example, may need to access a back-end database, while some may need CPU-intensive processing. Information about the coarse-grained "cost" of a request execution can help in an approximate comparison of the resource consumption of different requests. Usually such cost is specified on the basis of request type. This choice has the following rationale. Processing times for individual requests in typical Internet services can vary widely by as much as two-to-four orders of magnitude. However, there tends to be much more variation across request types than for requests within the same type but with different request parameters [32, 45].

Coarse-grained request resource utilization (request execution cost) can be specified by the service provider in the form of abstract *resource consumption units* (called *computational quantums* in [32]). However, such *static* specification can be quite inaccurate for the following reasons. First, request execution times tend to depend on actual user load — request processing times under heavy load are much higher that those measured in isolation. Second, execution of complex SQL queries in the database, especially those involving merging and sorting, depend on the volume of the data processed, which may vary considerably during service lifetime. An alternative approach, which we adopt in this work, is to specify request execution cost as the average request processing time of the requests of certain type. This approach is also attractive because it allows automated collecting and updating the required information through online request profiling in real time.

3.2.2 Request reward

Service providers of business critical services are interested in boosting service revenues. However, different user sessions make different contribution to the profit attained by the service. The specification of profit (or, generally speaking, "reward") brought by service requests is an opportunity for service providers to indicate which requests are more valuable, according to the service logic, or to indicate which requests are crucial for the service. This information may be used by server-side resource management mechanisms to preferentially allocate server resources to requests. Let's consider the following three examples.

- In the online shopping scenario introduced earlier (Section 1.1), the service provider might be interested in giving a higher execution priority to the sessions that have placed something in the shopping cart (potential *buyer* sessions), as compared to the sessions that just *browse* product catalogs, making sure that clients that buy something (and so — bring profit to the service) receive better QoS.

- For Internet services, some of whose web pages contain third party-sponsored advertisements, the service provider's profits may (directly) depend on the number of visits to these pages. Consequently, the service provider may wish to provide better QoS to the sessions that visit these pages more often.

- For many services whose client interactions involve different length sessions, service profit may be defined in terms of the number of sessions that visit a distinguished "success" page. In such cases, the service provider may prefer shorter sessions visiting the success page over longer ones, because it will be able to serve more of them.

It is the service provider's responsibility to define the *reward* function associated with the session. The model we adopt in this study is simple yet general enough to encompass several possible applications: a reward value is defined for every request type of the service. The reward of the session is the sum of rewards of the requests in the session. The reward counts only if the session completes successfully.

To illustrate the reward formulation, let us define reward functions for the three example scenarios presented above.

- In the on-line shopping scenario the profit of the service is reflected by the volume of items sold. One way to define a reward function for the on-line store service is by assigning a reward value of 1 for the Add to Cart request (see Fig. 3.2) — the shopping cart will contain as many items in it as the number of times the Add to Cart request was executed.

- In the example of third party-sponsored advertisements, the idea of reward specification is straightforward — assign each such web page a reward value based on the agreement between the service and the third party, e.g., based on how much the latter pays the former for a client's click on this page.

- In the example where the service provider wants to maximize the number of successful sessions the reward specification is done by assigning a reward value of 1 to the request corresponding to a visit to the "success" page.

3.3 Fine-grained server resource utilization

This service access attribute provides detailed information about how service requests are processed in the application server. The actual information about the way a request gets processed by the server may vary for different problems, QoS targets and metrics being optimized. Here are the examples of information that could be specified in this service access attribute and that could be useful in determining server resource utilization by service requests.

- Components invoked during a request's execution, their types and times spent in each component. As we discussed in Section 2.2.2, component invocation is a relatively expensive operation for the application server, so a requests's server resource consumption is directly affected by how many component invocations are involved in the execution of a given service request.

- Communication with auxiliary middleware services, such as JNDI naming service, Transaction Manager service, or JMS messaging service. This information may be used in assessing the request's resource consumption, in identifying the middleware services required to run on a given server node, and in identifying middleware component and performance bottlenecks.

- Datasources accessed by a request and times spent processing SQL directives. Processing complex database queries is a major performance bottleneck in modern data-centric Internet services, therefore

69

this information can be used in assessing the execution complexity of a request.

- Request's transactional behavior. As we discussed in Section 2.2.3, based on the request's transactional attributes and on the components' deployment policies, executing a method invocation may require exclusive access to the invoked component. This information may help in identifying the application's locking behavior and its lock bottlenecks.

The low-level information about how service requests are processed in the application server can be obtained through a fine-grained profiling of server-side request processing (made possible by componentized server architectures; see Section 2.2.2 for the discussion, and Section 3.5 for the description of our JBoss request profiling infrastructure), by statically analyzing the application structure (application source code and deployment descriptors), or by a combination of both approaches.

3.3.1 Request execution model with 2-level exclusive resource holding

In this section we present a model of request execution with 2-level exclusive resource holding (threads and DB connections) — an example of the actual specification and usage of information about fine-grained server resource utilization. We use this model for optimizing utilization of server resource pools (Chapter 5).

It is often the case that middleware server performance is limited by several "bottleneck" resources, that are *held exclusively* by a request for the whole duration or some significant portion of it (such as server threads or database (DB) connections), as opposed to low-level *shared* OS resources. In the absence of application errors, failing to obtain such a resource is the major source of request rejection.

We advocate and use a request execution model, where a request is rejected (with an explicit message) if it fails to obtain a critical server resource within a specified time interval. This approach is shared by a vast majority of robust server architectures that bound request processing time in various ways (e.g., by setting a deadline for request completion), as opposed to

70

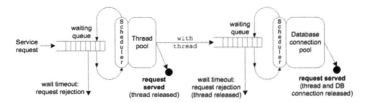

Figure 3.5: Request execution model with 2-level exclusive resource holding (threads and database connections).

a less robust approach, where a request is kept in the system indefinitely, until it is served (or is rejected by lower-level mechanisms such as TCP timeout). The former approach not only guarantees that a request is either served within a time limit or unambiguously rejected, but also helps to more efficiently free server resources of the requests that can not be handled due to the server capacity limitations.

Fig. 3.5 schematically illustrates our model of request execution and the flow of a request through the system. Requests compete for two critical exclusively-held server resources: server threads and DB connections; these resources are pooled by the web server and the application server respectively. If the timeout value for obtaining a thread or a DB connection expires, the request is rejected with an explicit rejection message. An acquired database connection is cached and is used exclusively by the request, until it is processed (the rationale and advantages of caching will be discussed in Section 5.3). When the request is processed, the thread and cached database connections are returned to their respective pools. Note that some requests do not require access to database(s), so they can be successfully served just by acquiring a server thread. For the purposes of this model we also make a simplifying assumption that there is a single database that stores the application data and that all the communication with the database required to process a service request can be made over a single DB connection, in other words, a request requires no more than one DB connection (see also the discussion in Section 5.3).

In this model of request processing, request execution time can be represented as follows:

$$t = w^{\text{THR}} + p + w^{\text{DB}} + q \tag{3.5}$$

where w^{THR} is the time waiting for a thread, p — time doing request processing before getting a DB connection, w^{DB} — time waiting for a DB connection, q — time processing the request with the DB connection cached. This latest time includes the time spent in making SQL queries, retrieving the results, processing them, and making all other request processing while the DB connection is cached by the request. Also note that in this work we treat the database as a black box.

In Chapter 5 we will show how this model of request execution with 2-level exclusive resource holding can be used to identify the optimal configuration of the thread and DB connections pools. More specifically, achieving this becomes possible with the knowledge of the values of p and q, which can be obtained through fine-grained profiling of request processing.

3.4 Data access patterns

This service access attribute contains information about how service requests access application data. The information specified at this level again varies for different problems, QoS targets and metrics being optimized, but typically it would specify the *read-write behavior* of a request with respect to the data it accesses, and information about whether this data is shared among multiple users. This service access attribute may also specify, based on the needs of a specific service management problem, more detailed information, for example, what segment(s) of application data is (are) accessed and what are the consequences of accessing this data. It may also specify how tolerable a certain request is to *application data quality* (see Section 1.1), this information may be used in managing data replication and caching.

Below we describe a concrete example of specifying information about data access patterns of service requests.

3.4.1 OP-COP-VALP model

In the problem of providing session data integrity guarantees (Chapter 6), information about the business-critical shared application data that the service provider needs to cover by data consistency constraints can not be automatically extracted from the application structure or code — it needs to be identified by the service provider. To this end, we propose a flexible model for specifying web session data consistency (integrity) constraints — the OP-COP-VALP model. This model draws its ideas from several areas of advanced transaction processing (Section 2.7.2), such as *semantics-based concurrency control* and *relaxed consistency* but is specifically tailored for the case of web sessions.

In the OP-COP-VALP model, potential shared data conflicts are identified by specifying pairs of *conflicting* service requests (operations): OPeration (OP in short) and Conflicting OPeration (COP in short). The relation is not symmetric apriori and means that COP *invalidates* OP, that is, the COP request changes some data, that was accessed or updated during the execution of an OP request by another session. One may also associate correlation Id(s) (corr.Id in short) with both the OP and the COP requests. corr.Id(s) is a (set of) value(s) that can be extracted from the parameters and the return value of the request. The OP and COP requests are considered *conflicting* if they come from different sessions (COP after OP) and their corr.Id(s) match (have a non-empty intersection as sets). For simplicity, one may think of OP and COP as READ and WRITE operating with associated conflict semantics. Let's consider two examples, taken from an online store application:

Example 1: Item Quantity:

OP: Add To Cart request, adding an item to the shopping cart
corr.ID: itemId, a parameter specifying the ID of the item added to the cart

COP: Commit Order request, finalizing the purchase
corr.ID(s): the set of itemIds of the items in the shopping cart

This example says that the Commit Order request conflicts with the Add

To Cart request if they involve the same item. Note that an item is added by a user to his shopping cart based on the information about its *price* and *available quantity*. Commit Order request decrements the available quantities of the items purchased, thus potentially invalidating the information previously presented to the users who added the corresponding items into their shopping carts.

Example 2: List Of Items:

OP: Search Items
corr.ID: category, a parameter specifying the category of items the user looks for

COP: Insert Item, a service request, which inserts an item into the product catalog
corr.ID: some request parameter that represents category of the inserted item

This example says that the Search Items request (which returns the set of items belonging to a particular category) is invalidated by the Insert Item request (which inserts a new item into the product catalog), if the inserted item belongs to the same category. This specification of a data conflict makes sense semantically, because after such an insertion, the result of the Search Items request would be different, now containing the newly inserted item.

Given this notion of conflicting operations, there are two ways to specify the data inconsistency that can be tolerated by the service:

1. The *Invalidation Distance* approach specifies the number of COP requests from other sessions that need to happen after the OP request, for that OP to become invalid. The intuition is that each COP changes the data to a certain (fixed) degree, so data inconsistency can be measured in terms of the number of COP requests. This measure of data inconsistency is somewhat analogous to the *Order Error* used in the TACT formulation [147].

2. The *Numerical Distance* approach associates a numerical value (NUM_VAL) with the OP request, as a function of the request parameters and the return value; and defines how the (correlated) conflicting

COP request changes this value. The latter is done by specifying a ChangeNumVal function for each COP operation. Examples shown below are given in the context of the conflicting operation pairs described earlier:

Example 1: Item Quantity:
NUM_VAL: the available quantity of the item put into the shopping cart in the Add To Cart request
ChangeNumVal(NUM_VAL) = NUM_VAL − i, where i is the quantity of the item in the purchase

Example 2: List Of Items:
NUM_VAL: the number of items returned by the Search Items request
ChangeNumVal(NUM_VAL) = NUM_VAL + 1

Numerical Distance makes possible specifying *absolute* and *relative* tolerable data inconsistency for the pairs of conflicting requests. Defining tolerable inconsistency through the Numerical Distance is analogous to the *Numerical Error* used in the TACT formulation [147].

As we discussed in Section 2.7.2, web sessions are user-driven and open-ended. There is no global *commit* for a web session, at which point the service logic could make sure that OPs of the session have not been invalidated, and consider the session ended. Additionally, in several situations, data consistency constraints for the session need only be satisfied if the session reaches a certain point. For example, in the buyer scenario one would want an item's price and quantity not to change substantially only if the user finally buys the item. Such events, when the service logic should *validate* a session's OPs, needs to be explicitly specified: in our model this is done by specifying VALidation Points (VALP in short). VALP is a service request with a reference to a set of previously defined OPs (if necessary, correlated through corr.Ids), that it *covers*. The logic is that identified OPs need to be kept *valid* only for the time duration between the OP and VALP requests.

Abstracting application-specific data conflicts into the OP−COP−VALP model allows the application to delegate the responsibility for enforcing

75

desired data consistency constraints to the underlying middleware. Generic middleware mechanisms could enforce data consistency constraints working only at the level of the abstract OP-COP-VALP model, with mapping of requests to OPs, COPs and VALPs, and other information specified by the service provider. This separation is consistent with the middleware concept of offloading functionality from the application code to the underlying server environment, and additionally permits *dynamic adaptation* of concurrency control policies to changes in parameters of service usage, in order to maximize the specified metric.

We use the OP-COP-VALP model later in this book to provide session data integrity guarantees (Chapter 6).

3.5 Request profiling infrastructure

Tracing user requests is a well known technique and is widely used in computer systems for various purposes, such as accounting, debugging, and performance analysis. The feature of request logging is available on all mature web servers, however, the information traced by the standard request logging functionality has a very limited scope. In order to be able to gather more fine-grained information about request execution, we need an request profiling infrastructure, such as one used in a recent study [31] for problem determination and root cause analysis in dynamic Internet services.

In this section we present our request profiling infrastructure and describe its implementation in the JBoss/Jetty web application server. The implementation takes advantage of the microkernel architecture of JBoss (Section 2.3.1) and overall contributes to less than 1% of the server codebase. The infrastructure (as well as all other middleware mechanisms injected in JBoss) is implemented in a modular, extensible, and pluggable fashion with minimal, backward compatible, changes to the original application server code. We also show that performance overheads imposed by the infrastructure are rather small.

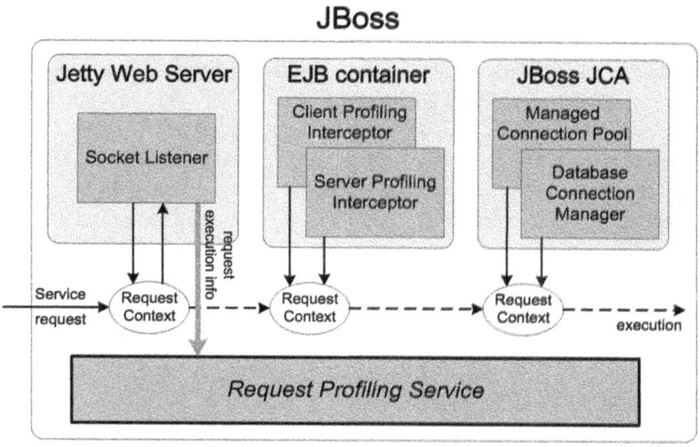

Figure 3.6: Architecture of the JBoss/Jetty profiling infrastructure.

3.5.1 JBoss instrumentation

Various JBoss/Jetty modules are augmented with additional functionality and execution hooks to gather information about service request execution. While a request is being processed, all the information associated with it is kept in the local *Request Context*, associated with the request through a dedicated `ThreadLocal` Java object (a request is executed by a single thread). When the request completes, this data is sent to the *Request Profiling Service*, where it is added to a server-wide in-memory service usage information storage. Fig. 3.6 schematically shows the architecture of the profiling infrastructure.

Request Profiling middleware service

The Request Profiling middleware service acts as a centralized storage of information about completed service requests. It is implemented as a JMX

MBean (Section 2.3.1) in order to standardize access to it. The service keeps track of currently active sessions, as well as the aggregated information about recently completed service requests. The former is used to keep histories of session requests and inter-request times for currently active sessions, while the latter is used to extract various parameters of service usage from the history of recent requests executed against the service.

Request profiling in JBoss/Jetty is performed at all three Java EE tiers (Section 2.2.1). The profiling functionality is injected in a modular and pluggable fashion — by substituting certain functionality modules with ones also augmented with the profiling execution hooks. Only absolutely necessary changes were made to the original JBoss/Jetty code, which are backward compatible with the original server configuration.

Web tier profiling

Request profiling at the web tier is performed by the modified Jetty HTTP/web server. It is used to gather high-level request flow information about incoming client requests, which are classified by their *type* (based on the URL pattern) and session affiliation. To inject profiling functionality, we substituted the default Jetty's *Socket Listener* module, which listens for incoming user requests on a predefined TCP/IP port and performs server thread pooling, by an augmented socket listener implementation, which for each request creates the *Request Context* object and associates it with the request's thread (see also Section 4.5 for other changes introduced to the *Socket Listener* module). When a request completes, the information accumulated in the request context is sent to the Request Profiling service.

EJB tier profiling

Profiling at the EJB tier is performed by adding two JBoss EJB interceptors (Section 2.3.2) — *Client Profiling Interceptor* and *Server Profiling Interceptor* (each at the client and the server side, correspondingly), which record in the request context the information about components and methods invoked. The interceptors are also responsible for propagating the request context between the JVMs by putting it in the serializable part of the

78

invocation object, that travels over the wire, in case of a remote invocation.

Data tier profiling

JBoss uses the Java Connector Architecture (JCA) [115] to integrate the relational datasources. JCA allows the application server to pool database connections and to manage their transactional and security aspects in a standardized fashion. We injected the profiling functionality into the data tier by modifying the *Database Connection Manager* and *Managed Connection Pool* modules (see also Section 4.5 for other changes introduced to these modules). This allowed us to gather information about how database connections are assigned to requests and record various connection management events, e.g., when connections are requested from the pool, granted, closed and returned to the pool (Section 2.2.2). We do not profile how specifically DB connections are used by requests (i.e., what JDBC queries are executed). Such more detailed information can only be obtained with additional profiling hooks injected into the database-specific JDBC driver code. However, information gathered by our profiling mechanisms is sufficient for the server resource management mechanisms we describe in Chapter 5.

3.5.2 Gathering and analyzing the information

The Request Profiling middleware service not only gathers the information about recent service requests, but also provides mechanisms to manage this information and methods to extract parameters of service usage that we are interested in.

To keep track of only *recent* service usage, we implement an information gathering mechanism where events are stored in so-called *shifting epochs*. A currently *open* epoch records events (e.g., new session arrivals) either for a specified time interval or until it accumulates a certain number of events, after which this epoch *closes*, a new one opens and starts to record events, and the oldest epoch is discarded. This mechanism simplifies phasing out the aging epochs, imposes a limit on the memory used for storing the information, and also reduces data management overheads of recording an event (one does not need to discard the oldest event on every event arrival).

To extract various service usage parameters (e.g., average session inter-request time) we perform statistical analysis of the accumulated data. Each request for a parameter estimate indicates the number of recent epochs to be used for it, and each calculated parameter estimate is accompanied by the *confidence interval* with confidence level value of 95%, computed using the Student's T-test [102]. The confidence interval contains the actual value that we are trying to estimate with a probability of 95%. Based on the specific problem at hand, a computed parameter estimate can be deemed *invalid*, if its confidence interval is larger than a predefined threshold (e.g., ± 0.01, or $\pm 10\%$ of the estimated value). In this case, the parameter estimate can be discarded or recomputed taking into account a greater number of epochs (and a greater number of events), which will likely decrease the computed confidence interval.

3.5.3 Performance overheads of the profiling infrastructure

To evaluate the performance overheads that our profiling infrastructure imposes we conducted a series of experiments with two server configurations with the TPC-W application deployed on them: (1) original JBoss/Jetty application server and (2) JBoss/Jetty augmented with our profiling infrastructure.

The server environment for these tests consisted of two dedicated 1GHz dual-processor Pentium III workstations (one with JBoss/Jetty web application server, another with MySQL database server), connected by a high-speed LAN. A separate workstation was used to produce artificial session-oriented user load, with different λ, the rate of new session arrivals (Section 3.1.4). In order to better evaluate the overheads of the profiling infrastructure, we used the TPC-W application configuration with the smallest database population size, and therefore with the highest sustainable request throughput: NUM_EBS = 1, NUM_ITEMS = 100 (Section 2.4.1). For the same purpose, we used in-memory (HEAP) database tables in the MySQL database.

In the experiments we measured average request response times and

Table 3.1: Comparative performance of JBoss/Jetty web application server augmented with the profiling infrastructure (**orig.**: original server architecture, **prof.**: augmented with the profiling infrastructure).

User load (in λ)	Average request response time (ms)		CPU utilization		Memory utilization (MB)	
	orig.	**prof.**	**orig.**	**prof.**	**orig.**	**prof.**
$\lambda = 1$	40	52	9.7%	9.9%	104	125
$\lambda = 2$	61	75	25.9%	27.4%	109	135
$\lambda = 3$	83	104	32.0%	35.9%	114	143
$\lambda = 4$	127	201	40.3%	45.1%	142	164
$\lambda = 5$	187	320	57.4%	64.2%	154	173
$\lambda = 5.5$	670	n/a	68.8%	n/a	160	n/a

CPU and memory utilization. The latter two parameters were only measured for the JBoss/Jetty server, because MySQL server performance did not depend on the presence of the JBoss/Jetty profiling infrastructure. In both tested server configurations, the MySQL database server was the performance bottleneck. The results of the experiments are shown in Table 3.1.

The presence of the profiling infrastructure decreased the maximum sustainable session throughput, but only slightly ($\lambda = 5.5$ was the approximate maximum session throughput for the original server configuration, while $\lambda = 5$ — for the server augmented with the profiling infrastructure). As the results show, CPU and memory overheads are small and are consistent for various user loads. Request response times for the server with the profiling infrastructure are only marginally higher, if the server operates well below maximum sustainable user load. The overhead margin becomes higher as the load approaches server capacity, but under such load the server is anyway showing deteriorating performance, as request response times for both the original JBoss/Jetty server configuration and the one with the profiling infrastructure skyrocket.

3.6 Chapter summary

In this chapter we have presented four related groups of *service access attributes*, that correspond to different levels of service usage information, ranging from high-level structure of user sessions, to low level information about resource consumption by different request types. We have described specific examples of information belonging to different service access attributes and have shown how this information can be obtained and abstracted into specific models of service usage and resource utilization, used in this book.

We have also presented our request profiling infrastructure that we implemented in the Java EE application server JBoss for automated gathering of service usage information. We have described how execution of service requests is profiled at different application tiers, and how the obtained information is gathered, stored and analyzed. The results of the experiments evaluating relative performance of the original JBoss server and JBoss augmented with the profiling infrastructure show that performance overheads of using the infrastructure are marginal.

Chapter 4

Maximizing Reward Brought by Internet Services

This chapter focuses on the problem of maximizing reward brought by Internet services, which was introduced earlier in Section 1.2.1. In Sections 4.1 and 4.2 we formulate the problem and present our approach to solving it. Section 4.3 briefly reiterates over the models used and the assumptions made, while also providing some additional details. In Section 4.4 we describe the proposed reward-driven request prioritization (RDRP) techniques. Section 4.5 details the middleware support required by the RDRP mechanisms and Section 4.6 presents our evaluation methodology and experimental results.

4.1   Problem formulation

In a typical setting a web application server hosting an Internet service processes incoming user requests on a first-come-first-served (FIFO) basis. Although this approach provides fair access to the service for all clients, it does not work as well if the service operates under overload conditions, whether such conditions are steady or transient (as a result of bursty client behavior). In such situations, clients see increased response times and their requests (and the containing sessions) may get rejected, which leads to user frustration, and as a consequence, to lowered usage of the service and reduced service revenues.

Consequently, modern-day services may contain one or more server-side mechanisms to deal with such overload situations. Session-based admission control (Section 2.6.1) admits only as many sessions as can be served by the service. More complex service differentiation mechanisms (Section 2.6.2) have also been used to provide stable QoS guarantees (e.g., request throughput, response times) to different client groups, based on prenegotiated Service-Level Agreements (SLAs). Common to such schemes is the consideration that the QoS received by a client is determined upfront by his association with a client group or by his service membership status.

Although they offer better performance than FIFO scheduling, the above schemes fall short of delivering the best performance in many important scenarios. In particular, a service provider often encounters situations where it makes sense to differentiate among clients based on the (dynamic) activities these clients perform in a session, rather than on their (static) identity, in order to boost service revenues, or for other application-specific goals. Let's consider the following three examples.

- In the online shopping scenario introduced earlier, the service provider might be interested in giving a higher execution priority to the sessions that have placed something in the shopping cart (potential *buyer* sessions), as compared to the sessions that just *browse* product catalogs, making sure that clients that buy something (and so — bring profit to the service) receive better QoS.

- For Internet services, some of whose web pages contain third party-sponsored advertisements, the service provider's profits may (directly) depend on the number of visits to these pages. Consequently, the service provider may wish to provide better QoS to the sessions that visit these pages more often.

- For many services whose client interactions involve different length sessions, service profit may be defined in terms of the number of sessions that visit a distinguished "success" page. In such cases, the service provider may prefer shorter sessions visiting the success page over longer ones, because more of them could be served.

These examples are unified by the idea that the service may benefit from providing better QoS to sessions, which bring more *profit* (give more *reward*), where the notion of profit or reward is defined in an application-specific fashion. What is important is that the information about the client's possible usage of a service (and its associated contribution to service reward) is not encoded in any static profile, so application-logic-independent SLA-based service differentiation approaches are not as beneficial here.

Instead, to be able to provide better QoS to the sessions that bring more reward, the service provider now needs to predict the behavior of a client. If the client is a returning customer and his identity can be determined (e.g., using HTTP cookies), than decisions on QoS provided to this client can be based on the history of his service usage (e.g., history of previous purchases). However, the success of this per-client *history-based approach*, is, not unexpectedly, highly dependent on the correlation between the past and the future behavior of a client, and may not work well if such a correlation is absent or weak.

4.2 Approach

Instead of focusing on individual client behavior, we advocate the approach of predicting a session's activities by associating it with aggregated client behavior or broader service usage patterns, obtained for example through online request profiling. Specifically, we introduce *Reward-Driven Request Prioritization* (RDRP) mechanisms that try to maximize reward attained by the service, by dynamically assigning higher execution priority values to the requests whose sessions are likely to bring more reward. Our methods compare the sequence of a session's requests seen so far with aggregated information about client behaviors, and use a Bayesian inference analysis to statistically predict the future structure of a session, and so — the reward the session will bring and the execution cost it will incur. The predicted reward and execution cost values are used to compute each request's priority, which is used in scheduling "bottleneck" server resources, such as server threads and database connections, to incoming client requests.

We have implemented our proposed methods as a set of middleware mechanisms, which are seamlessly and modularly integrated in the open-source Java web application server JBoss (Section 2.3). Our profiling infrastructure performs automatic real-time monitoring of client requests to extract parameters of service usage and to maintain the histories of session requests. It also performs fine-grained request profiling to identify execution times for different service request types. This information is used to compute request priorities, which in turn influence queueing behavior for various application server resources. We evaluate our approach on the TPC-W benchmark application (Section 2.4.1) using CBMG-based web workloads (Section 3.1.2), and compare it with both the session-based admission control and per-client history-based approaches.

4.3   Models and assumptions

Component-based Internet services are usually built as complex (and often distributed) software systems, consisting of several logical and physical tiers and accessing multiple backend datasources. We present our request prioritization algorithms in a simplified centralized setting however, to focus on the benefits of the proposed request prioritization techniques. We expect that the methods will show their utility in a distributed setting as well, where they can be independently applied at every system resource contention point that sees concurrent requests competing for server resources.

As everywhere throughout this book, we use the request execution model with 2-level exclusive resource holding (Section 3.3.1). Fig. 4.1 illustrates the logical model of web application server architecture and the flow of a request through the system. Requests compete for two critical exclusively-held server resources: server threads and database (DB) connections; these resources are pooled by the web server and the application server respectively. Scheduling of requests to available threads and DB connections is done according to the request priority set by the RDRP algorithm. The request with the highest priority is served first, with FIFO used as a tiebreak-

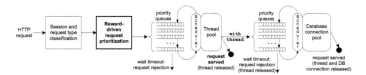

Figure 4.1: The logical model of web application server architecture.

ing policy. If a request is unable to obtain a thread (a DB connection) within a predefined time interval, it is rejected with an explicit message. Note that some requests do not require database access, so they can be successfully served just by acquiring a server thread. See Section 4.5 for information on how these pieces of functionality is implemented in the middleware.

Our RDRP algorithms work with the assumption that information about the request flow structure is known. Specifically, we assume that the workload consists of K CBMGs: $CBMG_1$, $CBMG_2, \ldots, CBMG_K$ (Section 3.1.2). The probability of a session having the structure of $CBMG_k$ is p_k, $\sum_{k=1}^{K} p_k = 1$. For the session of structure $CBMG_k$, the probability of transition from state i to state j is $p_{i,j}^k$.

It is the service provider responsibility to define the *reward* function associated with the session. The model we adopt in this book was described in Section 3.2.2: a reward value is defined for every request type of the service. The reward of the session is the sum of rewards of the requests in the session. The reward counts only if the session completes successfully.

The coarse-grained resource utilization of a session is specified in terms of the *relative request execution cost* $cost_i$ for each request type i (Section 3.2.1). Information about the relative execution costs permits the RDRP Bayesian inference algorithm to be able to make adequate predictions of future server resource consumption by a session. We define $cost_i$ as the average processing time of requests of type i, without the time spent waiting for a thread or a DB connection. This information is obtained through fine-grained on-line request profiling (Section 3.5).

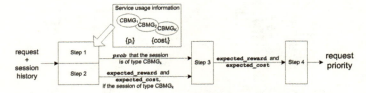

Figure 4.2: Logical steps of the RDRP method.

4.4 Reward-Driven Request Prioritization

The proposed RDRP mechanism works in the following way. For every incoming request, it looks at the sequence of requests already seen in the session and compares this sequence with the known CBMG structures of the session types comprising the user load. A Bayesian inference analysis estimates the probability that the given session is of type $CBMG_k$, for each $k = 1, \ldots, K$ (step 1). For each session type $CBMG_k$, the algorithm computes the values of *expected reward* and *execution cost*, resulting from the *future* requests of the session, assuming it had the structure $CBMG_k$ (step 2). This information is used to get the non-conditional values of expected reward and execution cost of the future session's requests (step 3). These values are used then to define the *priority* of the request (step 4), which governs the scheduling of available server threads and DB connections to incoming requests (see Fig. 4.1). The logical sequence of the RDRP algorithm steps is depicted in Fig. 4.2 and is explained in detail below.

Step 1. $\Pr\{CBMG_k \mid \text{req hist}\}$, the Bayesian estimate that the session is of certain type $CBMG_k$ (for a given history of session requests) is given by the following formula:

$$\Pr\{CBMG_k \mid \text{req hist}\} = \frac{\Pr\{\text{req hist} \mid CBMG_k\} \cdot p_k}{\sum\limits_{i=1}^{K} \Pr\{\text{req hist} \mid CBMG_i\} \cdot p_i} \quad (4.1)$$

where $\Pr\{\text{req hist} \mid CBMG_k\}$ is the probability of having a certain sequence of L requests $\{i_1, i_2, \ldots, i_L\}$ in a session of type $CBMG_k$ and is determined as

$$\Pr\{\text{req hist} \mid \text{CBMG}_k\} = \prod_{j=1}^{L-1} p_{l_j,l_{j+1}}^k \qquad (4.2)$$

Timing parameters. In the basic Bayesian analysis of distinguishing among possible session types (equations (4.1) and (4.2)), we took into account only the CBMG state transition information. However, if session inter-request user think times differ for sessions of various CBMG types, than this additional information can be used in an attempt to make the Bayesian inference analysis more accurate. Imagine that we know the distribution of user think times for each CBMG session type comprising the load, in particular their PDF functions, $\text{PDF}_k(x)$, $k = 1, \ldots, K$ ($\text{PDF}_k(x) = \Pr\{\text{time} < x\}$, for CBMG_k), and that the observed session inter-request times are $t_1, \ldots, t_{L-1}$ (L is the number of requests seen in the session). Then equation (4.2) can be substituted with the following one:

$$\Pr\{\text{req hist}, t_1, \ldots, t_{L-1} \mid \text{CBMG}_k\} = \prod_{j=1}^{L-1} p_{l_j,l_{j+1}}^k \cdot \prod_{j=1}^{L-1} \text{PDF}_k(t_j) \cdot (\Delta t)^{L-1}$$

$$(4.3)$$

where the infinitesimal time interval Δt appears in the equation, because the session inter-request times have supposedly continuous distributions. When equation (4.3) is substituted in equation (4.1), the infinitesimal value $(\Delta t)^{L-1}$ appears in both the numerator and the denominator, and cancels each other out. We call the basic method "RDRP(state)", and the RDRP scheme that involves inter-request timing considerations "RDRP (state+time)".

Step 2. To compute $\text{rew\_exp}\{\text{CBMG}_k\}$, the value of reward expected from the session's future requests, assuming it is of particular type CBMG_k, we just need to know the expected number of future session requests, for each request type (i.e., the expected number of future visits to each of the session's CBMG states). This information, combined with the assumption that reward is brought by individual requests allows us to compute the expected reward for the session. The expected number of future visits to a

CBMG state is a Markov property of the CBMG and is determined only by the current state (i.e., by the current request) and the CBMG's state transition probabilities. For example, in our sample TPC-W shopping scenario, where reward is brought by the Add To Cart request (Section 3.2.2), we have to compute A_i — the expected number of future visits to the Add To Cart state, if the current state is i. These values are determined by a set of linear equations, involving CBMG transition probabilities and can be computed mechanically [89]. For the sample TPC-W CBMG structure shown in Fig. 4.3, the values of A_i are given by the following expressions:

$$
\begin{aligned}
A_{\text{register}} &= A_{\text{buy\_req}} = A_{\text{buy\_conf}} = 0 \\
A_{\text{search}} &= \frac{P_{i,a}P_{s,i}}{(1-P_{s,s}-P_{s,c}P_{c,s})\cdot(1-P_{i,i}-P_{i,a}P_{a,i})-P_{i,s}P_{s,i}-P_{i,a}P_{a,s}P_{s,i}} \\
A_{\text{add}} &= A_{\text{search}} \cdot \left(P_{a,s} + \frac{P_{a,i}\cdot(1-P_{s,s}-P_{s,c}P_{c,s})}{P_{s,i}} \right) \\
A_{\text{item}} &= A_{\text{search}} \cdot \frac{1-P_{s,s}-P_{s,c}P_{c,s}}{P_{s,i}} \\
A_{\text{cart}} &= A_{\text{search}} \cdot P_{c,s} \\
A_{\text{home}} &= A_{\text{search\_e.c.}} = \frac{(1+A_{\text{add}})\cdot P_{ie,a}P_{se,ie}}{(1-P_{se,se})\cdot(1-P_{ie,ie})-P_{ie,se}P_{se,ie}} \\
A_{\text{item\_e.c.}} &= A_{\text{search\_e.c.}} \cdot \frac{1-P_{se,se}}{P_{se,ie}}
\end{aligned}
$$

We refer the reader to the original work [89], where the notion of CBMG was introduced and the CBMG apparatus for extracting various CBMG's Markov properties was developed. The values of expected execution cost from the session's future requests are computed in a similar way.

Step 3. The (non-conditional) values of expected reward and execution cost of the future session's requests are computed as a linear combination of the corresponding conditional values (i.e., for specific CBMG session types) weighted with the probabilities that the session is of that particular type:

$$
\text{rew\_exp} = \sum_{k=1}^{K} \text{rew\_exp}\{\text{CBMG}_k\} \cdot \Pr\{\text{CBMG}_k \mid \text{req hist}\}
$$

$$
\text{cost\_exp} = \sum_{k=1}^{K} \text{cost\_exp}\{\text{CBMG}_k\} \cdot \Pr\{\text{CBMG}_k \mid \text{req hist}\}
$$

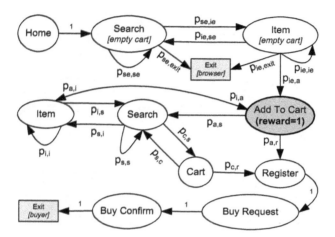

Figure 4.3: The graph structure of the CBMG used to represent our TPC-W browsing and shopping scenario.

Step 4. The underlying idea of request prioritization is very simple — give higher priority to requests from sessions that are expected to bring more reward, while consuming less server resources. We use two different schemes to define request priority — one takes into account the cost of the requests seen in the session (we call this scheme RDRP-1), and the other (RDRP-2) does not:

$$\text{priority}_1 = \frac{\text{rew\_attained} + \text{rew\_exp}}{\mathbf{cost\_incurred} + \text{cost\_exp}} \tag{4.4}$$

$$\text{priority}_2 = \frac{\text{rew\_attained} + \text{rew\_exp}}{\text{cost\_exp}} \tag{4.5}$$

rew_attained and cost_incurred are the reward and the execution cost of the requests already seen in the session. In Section 4.6.2 we motivate the differences in the two priority formulations and compare their performance.

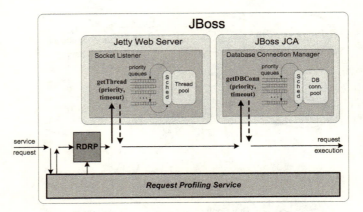

Figure 4.4: Middleware infrastructure supporting the RDRP mechanisms.

4.5 Middleware infrastructure

We have implemented the RDRP methods as a set of middleware mechanisms, which are seamlessly and modularly integrated in the open-source Java web application server JBoss (Section 2.3). Fig. 4.4 shows the middleware infrastructure supporting the RDRP mechanisms.

The *Request Profiling Service* (Section 3.5) performs automatic real-time monitoring of client requests to extract parameters of service usage and to maintain the histories of session requests. It also performs fine-grained profiling of request processing by the server. This information is used to periodically update the values of relative request execution cost $cost_i$ in the RDRP algorithm, defined as the average request processing time, without the time spent waiting for a thread or a DB connection.

After the initial processing of an incoming HTTP request and determining its type and session identity, the request is assigned the priority value computed by the *RDRP module*, according to the algorithms described in Section 4.4 and utilizing the service usage information gathered by the Request Profiling Service.

92

Request priorities are used for scheduling of requests to the available server threads and DB connections. The request with the highest priority is served first, with FIFO used as a tiebreaking policy. To enable such prioritized scheduling, necessary changes have been introduced into the JBoss' *Socket Listener* module, which performs pooling and scheduling of threads, and into the *Database Connection Manager* module, which performs pooling and scheduling of DB connections. Additional functionality is put in place to enable the robust request execution model with explicit request rejections (Section 3.3.1). Default timeout values for obtaining a thread and a DB connection are set to be 10s. If this timeout expires, the request is rejected with an explicit message.

4.6 Experimental evaluation

We start by describing the experimental setup and then present an evaluation of RDRP against alternative server-side schemes for managing application server resources.

4.6.1 Experimental setup

Server configuration

As was stated earlier, we present our RDRP algorithms in a simplified centralized setting in order to focus on the benefits of the request prioritization techniques. Our experimental infrastructure consists of a JBoss web application server and a separate database server, each running on a dedicated 1GHz dual-processor Pentium III workstation, connected by a high-speed local-area network (Fig. 4.5). A separate workstation is used to produce client load and to gather statistics.

We use MySQL version 4.1.1 with transactional InnoDB tables, for the database server. The database is treated as a black box and its configuration is kept default, with the exception of switching off database query caching.[1]

---

[1] This was done intentionally to eliminate the effects of repeated request patterns in the synthetic workload, which resulted in non-uniform request processing performance in the presence of database query caching.

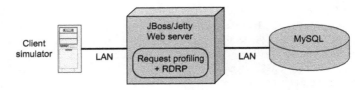

Figure 4.5: The server configuration used in the RDRP experiments.

We set the size of the server thread pool and the DB connection pool to 70 and 30 respectively (see Fig. 4.4).

TPC-W application

We test the request prioritization mechanisms on the sample TPC-W benchmark application (Section 2.4.1). The TPC-W database population parameters, which influence application performance, are chosen so as to achieve diverse execution complexity for different request types involved in the simulated sessions. We use the following values: NUM_ITEMS = 10000, NUM_EBS = 10. Table 4.1 shows average request response times for the TPC-W request types, when executed in isolation (only one request is processed by the server at a time). This information is presented to illustrate the relative execution complexity of requests, which range from very light (Register request, does not require database access and involves only simple application logic) to very heavy (Search request, performs execution of complex database queries). When executed concurrently, the requests see larger response times, because of queueing delays for critical server resources (threads and DB connections) and possible database contention.

As described in Section 3.2.2, in the online shopping scenario the profit of the service is reflected by the volume of items sold. In the TPC-W application, we assume that reward is brought by the Add To Cart request — the shopping cart will contain as many items in it as the number of times the Add to Cart request was executed. Therefore, we assign a reward value of 1 for the Add to Cart request and 0 to all other request types.

Table 4.1: Average request response times for the TPC-W request types, when executed in isolation.

Request type	Response time (ms)
Home	30
Search	450
Item	15
Add To Cart	20
Cart	5
Register	5
Buy Request	150
Buy Confirm	100

Client load

Our workload for the TPC-W application is a 50%/50% mix of the two CBMGs shown in Fig. 4.6 and Fig. 4.7. Both of the CBMGs use the same graph structure, but with different transition probabilities. The "Mostly Buyers" CBMG produces user sessions that tend to buy products, while the "Mostly Browsers" CBMG produces more browsing-biased sessions. This results in different frequencies of requests being invoked by the two kinds of sessions (Table 4.2). Note that not all "Mostly Buyers" sessions result in a purchase, and analogously, not all "Mostly Browsers" sessions just browse the product catalog. The 50%/50% mix of the given "Mostly Buyers" and "Mostly Browsers" sessions results in approximately 52% of sessions finishing with a purchase. This value may be higher than what most retail e-Commerce web sites see in real life, however such client behavior may be more characteristic of web sites providing online brokerage services, where a greater portion of user sessions results in completion of reward-bringing transactions of selling and buying stocks. We introduce this bias towards purchasing sessions to highlight the benefits of our request prioritization approach. However, we expect our methods to exhibit the same *relative* improvements even in workloads with fewer purchasing sessions.

New session arrivals and session inter-request user think times are mod-

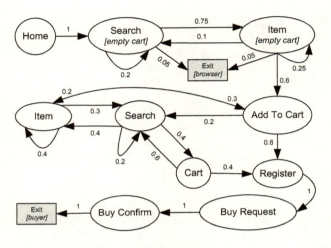

Mostly Buyers

Figure 4.6: The "Mostly Buyers" CBMG used for TPC-W workload.

eled as described in Section 3.1.4. We model session inter-request times as exponentially distributed with mean 5s for the "Mostly Buyers" sessions and 10s for the "Mostly Browsers" sessions. We use both "smooth" (Poisson) and "bursty" (using the B-model) arrival patterns for new session arrivals.

The maximum sustainable request rate of the server configuration under the resulted request mix is approximately 20 req/s, with the bottleneck being the MySQL database server.[2] The overall load produced on the system is determined by the arrival rate of new sessions. We use different values of this parameter to generate server overload as well as underload conditions

---

[2] This seemingly low server throughput is attributed, first, to the underprovisioned one generation old machines we were using for the experiments, and second, to the fact that we did not perform scrutinized database and TPC-W application tuning. However, we expect the relative performance improvements achieved by the RDRP methods to be similar in more powerful server environments.

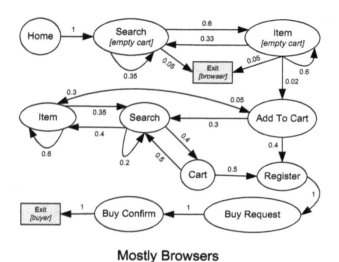

Mostly Browsers

Figure 4.7: The "Mostly Browsers" CBMG used for TPC-W workload.

and report the load measured as a percentage of the system processing capacity. Each test run generates approximately 5000 sessions, with statistics gathered from the middle 80% portion of the run time to cut off warm-up and cool-down regions.

Reported metrics

For each experiment, we measure the reward attained by the service (i.e., number of items bought by successfully completed sessions) and average request response times for sessions bringing different reward. We do not report the reward metric for the server underload situation, because in this situation all sessions complete successfully, and each request scheduling algorithm produces the same reward value. Where absolute values of reward are reported, they are counted *per incoming user session*. This is done to

Table 4.2: Average breakdown of TPC-W sessions by request types.

Request type	Session request breakdown	
	Mostly Buyers	Mostly Browsers
Home	10.0%	5.2%
Search	24.0%	36.0%
Item	24.7%	53.5%
Add To Cart	11.6%	1.2%
Cart	3.9%	1.1%
Register	8.6%	1.0%
Buy Request	8.6%	1.0%
Buy Confirm	8.6%	1.0%

show how close the employed algorithms are to the ideal situation, when all the *buying* sessions complete successfully, which brings the average per-session reward of **0.7** (this value is determined by the mix and the structure of the involved CBMGs shown in Fig. 4.6 and Fig. 4.7). In some of the experiments we show attained reward measured as a percentage of the reward value produced by the default FIFO request scheduling algorithm. This is done to emphasize the relative benefits that the request prioritization methods bring, compared with the default web application server policies.

4.6.2 Comparison of two priority schemes

We ran a set of experiments comparing the performance of the RDRP-1 and the RDRP-2 methods, corresponding to the two priority formulations in equations (4.4) and (4.5), under various load conditions. Figure 4.8 compares the performance of the two methods under different amounts of server overload, for "smooth" session arrivals. The RDRP-2 method outperforms RDRP-1 in all scenarios, but especially under high client load. To informally understand this outcome, consider a session that is just one or two steps away from its completion (e.g., it is in the Register state in the CBMG of Fig. 4.3). The RDRP-2 method, according to equation (4.5), gives this request a higher priority than RDRP-1 (equation (4.4)), because it does

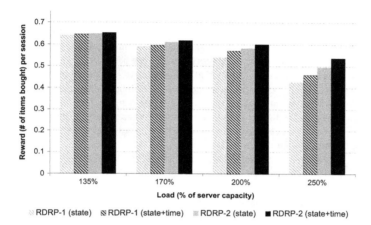

Figure 4.8: Comparison of benefits brought by the two flavors of the RDRP method.

not count the cost already incurred by the session. Consequently, under RDRP-1, the request might get rejected due to a low priority value, which will waste all the effort it took to bring the session to its nearly complete state. A careful examination of the logs produced during the experiments supports this explanation: the primary reason for the poor performance of RDRP-1 is the fact that some sessions are rejected with one or two requests left to complete the session, a phenomenon that never happens with RDRP-2. By ignoring the cost already incurred by the session, the RDRP-2 method appears to increase the likelihood of session completion as compared to its RDRP-1 counterpart. This also agrees with economics theory, which argues that *sunk costs* (i.e., costs that have already been incurred and which cannot be recovered, like cost_incurred in equation (4.4)), should not be taken into account when making rational decisions [138]. In the rest of the experiments we used only the RDRP-2 algorithm, and refer to it from now on as simply the RDRP method.

4.6.3 Imitating the "history-based" approach

As stated in Section 4.1, an alternative method to prioritize client requests to improve service reward is by using a per-client history-based approach. Broadly considered, such an approach models the behavior of any application-specific technique in which all requests of a session are assigned a constant priority value and are scheduled according to this priority. The priority assignment can have arbitrary logic, for example, it can be done in an attempt to predict the client's future behavior based on the history of the client's previous purchases, or it can be determined solely by the client's membership status.

The success of such approaches is determined, of course, by how good they are in predicting the client's behavior or, more precisely, the statistical correlation between assigned session priority and the actual reward brought by this session. To the best of our knowledge, prior work on workload characterization has not addressed such correlation in behavioral patterns (especially with the information that we need). We therefore employed the following scheme for producing a predefined correlation between the assigned session priorities and the actual rewards brought by the sessions. Each session announces in advance the reward it would bring, enabling the session prioritization mechanism to set the session's priority so that the statistical correlation (parameter c) between the assigned priorities and the sessions' rewards meets the predefined value. A value of $c = 1.0$ brings the best performance because the prioritization algorithm always assigns to requests from the session, a priority value in direct correspondence with the reward the session will bring.

4.6.4 Performance of RDRP

We compare the relative costs and benefits of RDRP mechanisms against the following alternative server-side request scheduling and overload protection methods:

- Default FIFO request scheduling with no request prioritization.

- Session-Based Admission Control (SBAC), which admits approxi-

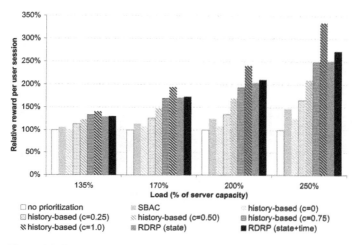

Figure 4.9: Reward relative to the default no-prioritization (FIFO) scheme, for the "smooth" client load.

mately as many sessions as can be processed by the server capacity; all of the admitted sessions are allowed to complete successfully. This method is used only in the server overload situation.

- The per-client "history-based" approach described in Section 4.6.3. We run five sets of experiments with $c = 0, 0.25, 0.5, 0.75$, and 1.0.

- Our RDRP(state) and RDRP(state+time) methods, described in Section 4.4.

Server overload

First, we evaluate the behavior of the methods in server overload situations. We run four sets of experiments, modeling loads of 135%, 170%, 200%, and 250% of server capacity, for both the "smooth" (Poisson) and

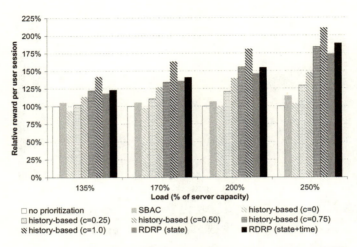

Figure 4.10: Reward relative to the default no-prioritization (FIFO) scheme, for the "high-bursty" client load.

"high-bursty" (B-model with $b = 0.75$) client loads (Section 3.1.4). Figures 4.9 and 4.10 show the reward attained by the service (number of items bought by successfully completed sessions, per user session), relative to the performance of the default FIFO request scheduling mechanism. Figures 4.11, 4.12, 4.13, and 4.14 show average request response times for sessions bringing different reward, for the "smooth" and "high-bursty" client loads. In each experiment, number of rejected requests, as expected, corresponds to the overload parameter of the client load used in the experiment. Response times of rejected requests are counted towards average request response times presented in the charts. Several conclusions can be drawn from the results of these experiments.

Reward attained. As expected, the default FIFO request scheduling policy shows the worst performance, because a request may get rejected anywhere in the session, which results in low successful session throughput.

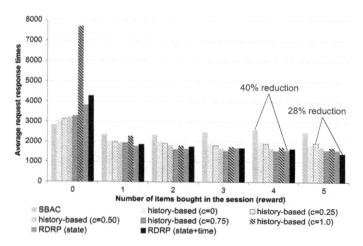

Figure 4.11: Average request response times for sessions that bring different reward, for "smooth" traffic, for the 135% server capacity overload situation.

The SBAC method works better, because it at least allows the sessions that have started to complete successfully, however it does not try to necessarily admit those sessions that bring the greatest reward. The history-based approach shows an increase in reward attained with an increase of the correlation between assigned session priorities and sessions' rewards. Note that even with values of $c = 0.25$, this method already outperforms the SBAC algorithm. Finally, both RDRP methods significantly boost reward attained by the service. The RDRP(state+time) method works slightly better than RDRP(state), because it takes into account the inter-request time differences between more-profitable "Mostly Buyers" sessions and less-profitable "Mostly Browsers" sessions and better distinguishes between them. The theoretically best history-based ($c = 1.0$) method, of course, shows the best performance, however the history-based approach matches

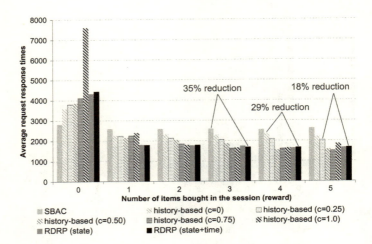

Figure 4.12: Average request response times for sessions that bring different reward, for "smooth" traffic, for the 170% server capacity overload situation.

the performance of the RDRP algorithms, only for values of $c \geq 0.75$.[3] The performance of all algorithms goes down, when the client load experiences bursty behavior, because under bursty conditions the queues for critical server resources are more susceptible to rapid build-ups, which results in higher rates of request rejections. However, the relative advantages of RDRP over the other methods stay the same.

Request response times. All algorithms that perform request/session prioritization, and manage to correctly guess (at least to a certain degree) the session's reward, decrease request response times for sessions that bring non-zero reward, as compared to the SBAC method. Both RDRP methods perform on par with the history-based approach for values of $c \geq 0.5$. For

---

[3] Whether such good prediction is possible in real life, remains an open question, due to the lack of publicly available information with such statistics.

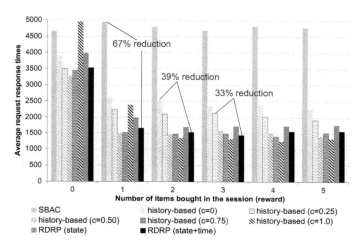

Figure 4.13: Average request response times for sessions that bring different reward, for "high-bursty" traffic, for the 135% server capacity overload situation.

the "smooth" client load, the RDRP algorithms reduce response times by up to 40% compared to SBAC, and show up to 28% lower response times than the history-based approach with $c = 0$ and $c = 0.25$. For bursty client load, the difference is more pronounced: response times from the RDRP methods are lower than that from SBAC and the history-based approach with $c = 0$ and $c = 0.25$ by up to 72%, 45%, and 36%, respectively.

Note, that for "smooth" client load, the sessions with zero reward (i.e., *browsing* sessions) see significantly increased response times, when the history-based approach with $c = 1.0$ is applied (Figures 4.11 and 4.12). This happens, because with the history-based approach, all browsing sessions (48% of all sessions, see Section 4.6.1 for the explanation) get the same (zero) priority, because the priority is defined as the session's reward, while the remaining 52% of sessions get a higher execution priority. Being all stuck in a single lowest-priority queue (with a FIFO tiebreaking pol-

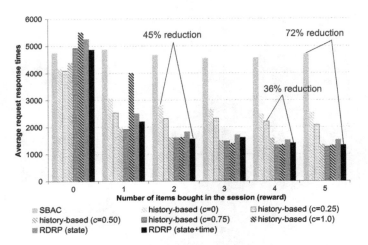

Figure 4.14: Average request response times for sessions that bring different reward, for "high-bursty" traffic, for the 170% server capacity overload situation.

icy), browsing sessions see higher rates of request rejections. This in turn produces higher response times for the session because a rejected request spends at least 10s in the system (before experiencing a timeout). Interestingly, this effect is reduced with bursty session arrivals (Figures 4.13 and 4.14).

Server underload

For server underload situations, we ran experiments with both "smooth" (Poisson) and bursty client loads. The Poisson-modeled web workload generated such a smooth flow of request arrivals, that all request scheduling algorithms showed more or less the same performance. This happened because the server queues for the critical resources (threads and DB connections) almost never built up, and requests were immediately scheduled

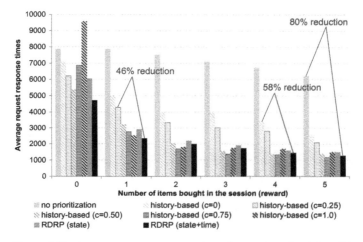

Figure 4.15: Average request response times for sessions that bring different reward, for "high-bursty" traffic, for the client load at 100% server capacity.

to available server threads and DB connections.

Experiments with the bursty client load showed very different behavior. Figures 4.15, 4.16, 4.17, and 4.18 show average request response times for sessions bringing different reward, for the two bursty client loads.[4] Several conclusions can be drawn from the results of these experiments.

The RDRP methods (as well as the history-based approaches) decrease request response times for the sessions that bring non-zero reward. This happens because with bursty arrivals (unlike the smooth arrival case described above), the queues for the critical server resources (server threads and DB connections) occasionally build up, and the request prioritization

---

[4] The experiments labeled as "100% of server capacity" were actually ran at a rate slightly lower than the server capacity, which experienced slight variations because of the non-deterministic behavior of the web application server. This ensured that our experiments did not slide into the overload mode of server operation.

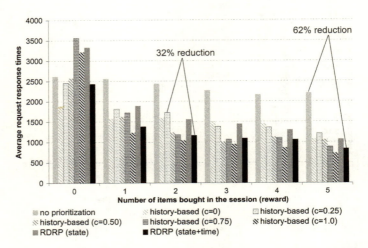

Figure 4.16: Average request response times for sessions that bring different reward, for "high-bursty" traffic, for the client load at 80% server capacity.

mechanisms minimize the queueing delays seen by the sessions that bring more reward by assigning their requests higher priorities. For "high-bursty" traffic, the effects of request prioritization are visible for loads above approximately 70% of server capacity (we show only experiments with the load of 100% and 80% of server capacity), while for the "low-bursty" traffic, the effects are visible for the load in the range of 85%–100% of server capacity.

As in the server overload situation, the performance of the RDRP methods is matched by the history-based approach only for values of $c \geq 0.5$. Under "high-bursty" traffic, RDRP outperforms the history-based method by up to 58% (for $c = 0$) and 46% (for $c = 0.25$). This advantage of RDRP over the history-based approach diminishes a bit under "low-bursty" traffic conditions (Figures 4.17 and 4.18). The default FIFO method performs

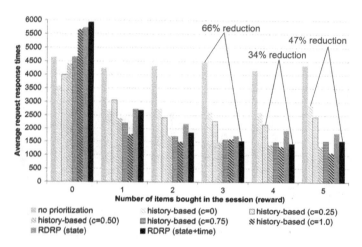

Figure 4.17: Average request response times for sessions that bring different reward, for "low-bursty" traffic, for the client load at 100% server capacity.

worst of all. It is interesting to note that even the history-based approach with $c = 0$, which is not supposed to ever correctly guess the session's reward, gives lower response times (for all reward values, including 0) than the default FIFO request scheduling scheme.

To our understanding, this behavior happens for the following reason. The request scheduling algorithm we adopt to imitate a history-based approach with $c = 0$ works by uniformly assigning priorities to sessions as integer values in the range of 0 to 100 (this process does not correlate with the session reward, therefore corresponds to $c = 0$). Some sessions get higher priorities than the other, and all sessions are uniformly sorted into a discrete number of priority buckets. Unlike the FIFO scheduling case, where all requests have to wait in one long queue produced by a traffic burst, the uniform session prioritization scheme permits some sessions to sneak ahead of other sessions. This perturbs the waiting times seen by re-

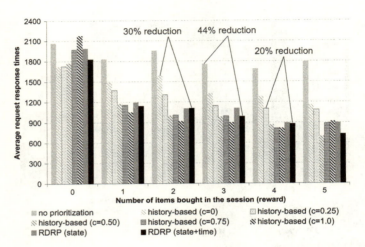

Figure 4.18: Average request response times for sessions that bring different reward, for "low-bursty" traffic, for the client load at 85% server capacity.

quests sufficiently so as to achieve an average response time lower than that seen by the FIFO case.

4.7 Chapter summary

In this chapter we have presented *Reward-Driven Request Prioritization (RDRP)* — a server-side resource management mechanism, which maximizes the reward attained by an Internet service by dynamically assigning higher execution priorities to the requests whose sessions are likely to bring more profit (or any other application-specific reward) to the service. The mechanisms work in an application-independent manner, utilizing the information exposed by the *request flow* (Section 3.1) and *coarse-grained resource utilization and reward* (Section 3.2) service access attributes. Namely, the mechanisms use the information about the request structure of user sessions, relative request execution costs, and "rewards", for requests of different types. We implemented the proposed methods as pluggable middleware mechanisms in the Java EE application server JBoss (Section 2.3), and tested them on the TPC-W benchmark application (Section 2.4.1).

Our experiments showed that RDRP techniques yield benefits in both underload and overload situations, for both smooth and bursty client behavior, against state-of-the-art alternatives such as session-based admission control and history-based session prioritization approaches. In the situation of service underload, the proposed mechanisms gave better response times for the clients that brought more reward. In the situation of service overload, the mechanisms ensured that sessions that brought more reward were more likely to complete successfully and that the aggregate profit attained by the service increased compared to other solutions. Additionally, we showed that the history-based approach matched performance of our RDRP mechanisms only if the correlation between the clients' past and future behavior reached the mark of 75% for the reward attained, and 50% for the request response times.

Chapter 5

Optimized Utilization of Server Resource Pools

This chapter focuses on the problem of optimizing utilization of Web application server resource pools, a topic introduced earlier in Section 1.2.2. In Sections 5.1 and 5.2 we formulate the problem and present our approach to solving it. Section 5.3 presents the request execution model with 2-level exclusive resource holding, which forms the basis for the techniques described in this Chapter. In Section 5.4 we describe the method for computing the optimal number of Web application server threads and database connections assuming this model, and Section 5.5 presents our evaluation methodology and experimental results.

5.1 Problem formulation

Modern component middleware are complex software systems that expose to service providers several mechanisms that can be independently tuned to improve server performance and optimize server resource utilization. The middleware layer itself rarely has control over low-level OS mechanisms, such as CPU scheduling and memory management. Instead, it provides control over higher-level resources, such as threads, database connections, component containers, etc. Some of these resources can be shared among concurrent user requests, but some are *held exclusively by a request* for the duration of its execution (or some significant part of it). Therefore, such non-shared resources become *bottleneck points*, and failure to obtain such a resource constitutes a major portion of request rejections under high load or overload conditions. Optimizing the utilization of these resources therefore becomes a high priority goal for the service provider.

The most important of such exclusively held server resources in Java EE-like component frameworks are server threads and database (DB) connections. The application server creates and pools a limited (predefined) number of threads and DB connections and schedules them to the incoming user requests. The pooling mechanism avoids expensive operations for creating and closing of these server resources (Section 2.2.2). The main question that the service provider (or the system administrator) faces in this context is *what is the optimal number of threads and database connections* that achieve the highest request throughput? Using more threads and database connections allows for increased execution parallelism, but may result in degraded performance due to thread context switching and increased data and locking contention in the database. The task of identifying the optimal number of threads and database connections is further complicated by the fact that for different user loads, different configurations of the thread and database connection pools provide the optimal application performance. This happens because different sets of application components and middleware services are used to execute requests of different types. Some requests, for example, need to access a database (so they need to obtain a DB connection), while some don't (Section 2.2.3).

5.2 Approach

To come up with a solution to this problem, we propose a methodology that computes the optimal number of threads and DB connections for a given application, its server and database environment, and specific user load (request mix). The methodology is built on a model that we propose for request execution with 2-tier exclusive resource holding (1st tier — threads, 2nd tier — DB connections), and works as follows.

- First, a limited set of off-line experiments are conducted, where the

113

actual application (Internet service) and its server environment are subjected to an artificial user load. We use a different number of threads and DB connections for each test run, and only a subset of possible values for these resources is used throughout the experiments. During this series of "profiling tests", information about *fine-grained server resource utilization* is obtained through the instrumented profiling of request execution. More specifically, we are interested in the times spent by the requests of different types in the different stages of request processing.

- Second, the obtained values for these timing parameters (considered as functions of the number of threads and DB connections) are used as data points for *function interpolation* to get the values of these parameters for all possible combinations of the number of threads and DB connections.

- Third, under real operating conditions, the proposed request execution model takes as input these interpolated functions and the information about actual *request flow* (request mix), obtained through on-line request profiling, and computes the number of threads and DB connections, which provides the best request throughput, thus achieving optimal utilization of web server threads and DB connections.

We discuss and justify the request execution model with 2-level exclusive resource holding in Section 5.3, while in Section 5.4 we present in greater detail the three steps comprising the method for computing the optimal number of threads and DB connections.

5.3 Request execution and database connection caching

As we previously stated in Section 3.3.1, in this work we adopt the following model of request execution by the application server. Requests compete for two critical exclusively-held server resources: server threads and DB connections; these resources are pooled by the web server and the application server respectively. If the timeout for obtaining a thread or a DB

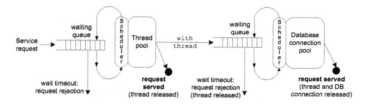

Figure 5.1: Request execution model with 2-level exclusive resource holding.

connection expires, the request is rejected with an explicit rejection message. An important detail is that the database connection obtained by a request *remains available for exclusive use by the request until the request is processed.* After that the thread and the database connection(s) cached by it are returned to their respective pools. Fig. 5.1 (taken from Section 3.3.1 and reproduced here for convenience) schematically illustrates the 2-level model of request execution and the flow of a request through the system.

The rationale for caching DB connections for the duration of request execution is as follows. To access a database a request obtains a database connection from the DB connection pool. After the required work (i.e., communication with the database) is done over this DB connection, the latter is returned to the pool. The particulars of the Java EE platform are such that a DB connection may be requested from the pool (and returned there) up to several dozen times during the execution of a single service request. For example, each business method invoked on an Entity EJB (Section 2.2) usually requires synchronization with the database (before or after the method invocation, or both). This results in a DB connection being requested (and returned) from the pool up to three times just during one EJB method invocation (if the synchronization is performed before the EJB method invocation, the additional EJB-specific `ejbFindByPrimaryKey()` method accounts for the third request [114]).

Most JDBC drivers (Section 2.2.1) additionally require that all database accesses on behalf of a single database transaction be performed over a single DB connection (to ease the implementation of transaction rollback and commit). To implement this requirement, application server JCA resource adaptors (Section 2.2.2), while perform DB connection pooling, cache DB connections for active transactions and return them to the pool only after the transaction completes. This approach, of course, reduces the number of times a DB connection is redundantly revoked and returned to the pool during the execution of a single request, but only for the requests associated with a transactional context. However, it is a common practice to make as few service requests transactional as possible, and usually only those that update back-end databases. Given that modern Internet services typically exhibit dominant non-transactional *read-only* data access patterns, the majority of service requests can not benefit from the approach of transaction-wide caching of database connections.

Similarly, in the situation of server overload (steady or transient), when DB connections become a scarce resource, concurrent requests compete for DB connections, experiencing queueing delays while trying to get them from the pool. The application performance can potentially deteriorate, because the same request has to get a connection from the pool several times. It not only increases request processing times, but also aggravates the situation by making requests that wait for a DB connection waste other exclusively held resources, such as server threads.

To alleviate this problem, we propose a DB connection pooling mechanism that caches database connections for the duration of the service request execution. This mechanism, in addition to caching DB connections for active transactions, caches at least one DB connection for each request that has requested a DB connection previously. Note that this does not guarantee that all the database activities for a single request can be performed over a single DB connection. If a request accesses two databases, or starts two transactions, or interleaves non-transactional activities with transactional ones, then these communications with the database(s) need to be performed over different DB connections. For the purposes of this chapter we however make a simplifying assumption that there is a single database that stores the application data and that all the communication with the database, required to process a single service request, can be made

116

over a single DB connection.

Of course, the approach of request-wide database connection caching may have its own drawbacks. Imagine, that between periods of communication with the database, a request performs some CPU-intensive processing of the application data. Returning the cached DB connection to the pool in this situation would allow some other requests to progress and would increase parallelism. While possible, we feel that this concern is not as relevant for the heavy database-centric applications that this work targets, such as TPC-W, Java Pet Store, and RUBiS (Section 2.4), where there is little data manipulation between accesses of the database.

We implement request-wide DB connection caching by augmenting the JBoss' Web/HTTP server Jetty and JBoss JCA resource adaptor with additional functionality (see Sections 2.2.2 and 2.3 for relevant background information). Section 5.5.2 presents the relative overheads and performance evaluation of the approach.

5.4 Computing the optimal number of threads and database connections

The goal of the proposed method is to compute the number of threads M and the number of DB connections N ($M \geq N$), that would maximize request (session) throughput, for a given incoming request mix. The information about the latter comes in the specification of V_i — average number of requests of type i in a session (Section 3.1.3). The method works with the assumption that the underlying hardware and middleware environments, as well as application configuration parameters are fixed.

In our 2-level model of request processing with request-wide DB connection caching (Sections 3.3.1 and 5.3), request execution time can be represented as follows:

$$t = w^{\text{THR}} + p + w^{\text{DB}} + q \tag{5.1}$$

where w^{THR} is the time spent by the request in waiting for a thread, p is the time the request spends on processing before getting a DB connection, w^{DB} is the time spent by the request in waiting for a DB connection, and

q is the time the request spends processing with a DB connection in its possession. The latter includes the time spent in making SQL queries, retrieving the results, processing them, and other request processing while the DB connection is cached by the request. In this chapter, we treat the database as a black box and do not track database activities performed over database connections. Note that for requests that do not access the database, $w^{\mathrm{DB}} = q = 0$.

The maximum sustainable request throughput depends on the values of p and q, which are different for different request types. The main assumption we make is that under the maximum server load, $p_i(M,N)$ and $q_i(M,N)$ — the average times spent processing requests of type i before obtaining a DB connection and with a DB connection, respectively — **depend only on M and N, and on the request mix** (the values of V_i).[1] We also assume that **the dependence of $p_i(M,N)$ and $q_i(M,N)$ on the incoming request mix (V_i) is very weak**, that is, the values of $p_i(M,N)$ and $q_i(M,N)$ change insignificantly when the request load parameters V_i stay *close enough* to their initial values. These assumptions are justified by the results of the initial experiments that we conducted while working on this problem.

In an optimal server configuration we would want to achieve a balanced utilization of server threads and database connections. This means that under maximum sustained user load, we would want all threads and DB connections to be fully utilized (they may be idle for some short periods of time, due to inevitable request burstiness, but the ideal situation is that all threads and DB connections are always "busy" processing requests). Having a noticeable number of idle threads or idle DB connections in situations where DB connections or threads (respectively) become the resource bottleneck is a waste of server resources and will cause performance degradation.

Assume for now, that we know the functions $p_i(M,N)$ and $q_i(M,N)$. With only N DB connections we can not process, on average, more than

$$\lambda_{\mathrm{DB}}(M,N) = \frac{N}{\sum_i V_i q_i} \qquad (5.2)$$

sessions per unit time, because incoming sessions have a certain number of

---

[1] Of course, they depend on the application configuration, the hardware and the middleware, but those are fixed.

118

requests that require database processing. For the same reason, with only M threads, we can not process more than

$$\lambda_{\text{THR}}(M,N) = \frac{M}{\sum_i V_i(p_i + q_i)} \qquad (5.3)$$

sessions per unit time, and this value is achievable if requests don't wait for DB connections (i.e., $w_i^{\text{DB}} = 0$). If we measure the throughput in number of sessions processed per unit time, than the maximum sustainable session throughput is given by the equation:

$$\lambda(M,N) = \min\{\lambda_{\text{DB}}(M,N), \lambda_{\text{THR}}(M,N)\}. \qquad (5.4)$$

The best configuration of server resource pools (i.e., the values of M and N) is the one, which maximizes the value in equation (5.4). The value in equation (5.4) has a global maximum *inside* a bounded region of possible values of M and N. Indeed, $\lambda_{\text{DB}}(M,M) > \lambda_{\text{THR}}(M,M)$, since if numbers of threads and DB connections are equal, threads present the "scarce" resource, because some requests do not require database access and DB connections may have idle periods. In comparison, $\lambda_{\text{DB}}(M,1) \leq \lambda_{\text{THR}}(M,1)$ (i.e., DB connections are the "scarce" resource), when M is big enough, because one DB connection can only do a limited amount of work. With M and N growing, the performance of the server deteriorates, and the values of both $\lambda_{\text{DB}}(M,N)$ and $\lambda_{\text{THR}}(M,N)$ go down. The situation when values of $\lambda_{\text{DB}}(M,N)$ and $\lambda_{\text{THR}}(M,N)$ are equal represents an optimal correspondence of the number of threads to the number of DB connections, which is a desirable situation. If sessions are coming with the rate of $\lambda_{\text{DB}}(M,N) = \lambda_{\text{THR}}(M,N)$ and if there is no burstiness in the request arrival pattern, then in an ideal processing environment all the requests will get served, with all the threads and DB connections being constantly busy processing the incoming requests.

These considerations lead us to the method, which consists of several steps schematically shown in Fig 5.2.

Step 1. Because of the assumptions we made earlier in this Section, we may consider $p_i(M,N)$ and $q_i(M,N)$ as two-dimensional functions, defined

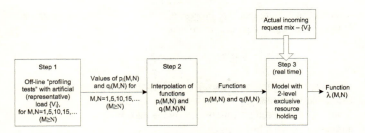

Figure 5.2: Logical steps of the method to compute the optimal number of server threads and database connections.

for the triangular grid of integer arguments (M,N), $M \geq N > 0$. The goal of this step is to obtain the values of p_i and q_i for some subset of possible values of M and N. These data points will be used for the interpolation of functions $p_i(M,N)$ and $q_i(M,N)$ on their domain. We choose the data points as a sub-grid of the functions' domain, for example: $M,N = 1,5,10,15,...$ $(M \geq N)$.

To obtain the values of p_i and q_i, for each interpolation point (M,N) we subject the actual server environment with an artificially induced user load slightly surpassing the server capacity. For this series of "profiling tests" we choose the parameters of the request mix (V_i) representative of the actual user load, or close to the load that we expect the system will see during its real-life operation. Due to the server overload conditions, either just one of the two, or both pooled server resources (threads and DB connections) will be used to their full capacity, and request queues will build up for threads, or DB connections, or both. However, if the overload is not too big, this overflow will be handled by the server in a graceful manner, because of our request processing mechanism that explicitly rejects requests, which can not obtain a thread or a DB connection within a predefined time interval. During these tests we obtain the values of $p_i(M,N)$ and $q_i(M,N)$ through fine-grained profiling of request execution, using our request profiling infrastructure (Section 3.5). Aborting some requests (and so — some sessions) will alter a bit the mix of served requests (as compared with the mix of requests *submitted to the system*), but as we stated earlier, the dependance of p_i and q_i on the request mix is very weak, so the measurements will produce very close to the correct values.

Step 2. The obtained data points for functions $p_i(M,N)$ and $q_i(M,N)$ are used for the interpolation of these functions on their domain ($M \geq N > 0$). To get a smooth interpolation we use the method of two-dimensional piecewise bi-cubic interpolation [72]. Instead of interpolating function $q_i(M,N)$ we interpolate the function $q_i(M,N)/N$ — this function turns out to be smoother and it is easier to interpolate than $q_i(M,N)$. It also has a meaningful interpretation — it is the inverse of the database throughput seen by requests of type i. We refer the reader to Section 5.5.3 for examples of interpolated functions $p_i(M,N)$ and $q_i(M,N)$.

Step 3. This step, unlike the first two ones, is performed in operating conditions and in real time, when the server environment is subjected to actual user load. The parameters of incoming request mix — the values of V_i — are obtained through online request profiling. As long as they stay *close enough* to the values used in the preliminary "profiling tests" (step 1), this method can be used to compute the optimal number of threads and DB connections. Substituting obtained values V_i and the values of $p_i(M,N)$ and $q_i(M,N)$, obtained in step 2, into the equations (5.2), (5.3), and (5.4), we get the value of maximum sustainable session throughput $\lambda(M,N)$, for every possible combination of M and N. Given that parameters M (the number of server threads) and N (the number of database connections) are discrete and have a limited (and rather small) set of possible values, it is possible to iterate over this set in order to, first, determine the optimal number of threads for a given number of DB connections, and vice versa, and second, find the pair of parameters (M,N) that achieve the highest session (request) throughput.

5.5 Experimental evaluation

In this section we present the evaluation of the proposed method for computing the optimal number of threads and database connections. Before proceeding to the evaluation of the method itself, we first present the details of the TPC-W application configuration used in the experiments, and second, evaluate the costs and benefits of the request-wide caching mechanism for database connections.

5.5.1 TPC-W configuration

In the standard TPC-W configuration with a typical database population, the performance bottleneck of our server environment is always the MySQL database server (Section 4.6.1). In order to evaluate our model, we need an application that would equally stress the application server and the database server. To achieve this, we choose TPC-W configuration parameters and make some changes to the TPC-W application code to make the application less database-centric and remove request processing focus from SQL query processing.

First, we use the smallest database population size: NUM_EBS $= 1$, NUM_ITEMS $= 100$ (see Section 2.4.1 for the details of TPC-W configuration and the description of service request types). Second, we use in-memory (HEAP) database tables in the MySQL database, which further speeds up SQL query processing. Third, we remove presentation of randomly chosen advertisements from the Home page, so that this request now does not require database access. And finally, we insert into the application code CPU-consuming code snippets, which are designed to imitate some CPU-intensive application server processing (for example, SSL processing) *before* the request obtains a DB connection (so it increases the values of p_i). These artificial code snippets produce different load for different request types (measured in *execution cycles*; each execution cycle is approximately 1 ms of execution time on our server environment, if request is executed in isolation): Home, Buy Request, Buy Confirm: 100 cycles, Search: 50, Add To Cart: 25, Item: 10, Cart, Register: 1. Table 5.1 shows p_i and q_i for the underloaded server (when only one request is executed at

Table 5.1: The values of p_i and q_i for the TPC-W application, in the under-loaded and "max-loaded" server environments ($M = N = 30$).

Request type	p_i under-loaded (ms)	q_i under-loaded (ms)	p_i "max-loaded" (ms)	q_i "max-loaded" (ms)
Home	97	0	235	0
Search	46	50	101	646
Item	9	9	26	311
Add To Cart	24	5	61	227
Cart	2	0	8	0
Register	2	0	7	0
Buy Request	94	59	205	940
Buy Confirm	93	112	230	1165

a time), and for the server stressed to its maximum load capacity ("max-loaded" server), with $M = N = 30$. It shows how p_i and q_i change when the load on the server increases.

5.5.2 Costs and benefits of request-wide database connection caching

In this section we evaluate the proposed mechanism for request-wide caching of database connections (Section 5.3) by comparing its performance with the performance of the default transaction-wide DB connection caching. We test our TPC-W application with various levels of bursty user load (Section 3.1.4) and measure the times that requests spend in different stages of their execution.

Figs. 5.3, 5.4, and 5.5 show the breakdown of request processing times for the Search, Buy Request, and Buy Confirm TPC-W requests respectively, for various levels of user load measured in percentage of server capacity. The left columns show results for our request-wide DB connection caching mechanism, while the right columns show results for the default transaction-wide DB connection caching mechanism. We distinguish among the following phases of request execution: *waiting for thread* (the time spent waiting for a thread to process the request), *with thread w/o DB*

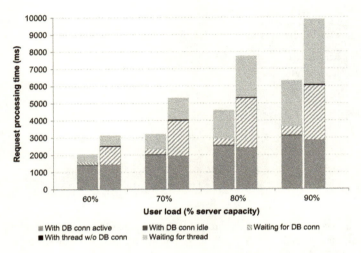

Figure 5.3: Breakdown of request processing time for the Search request (left column: request-wide DB connection caching, right column: transaction-wide caching).

connection (the time spent processing the request without holding a DB connection), *waiting for DB connection* (the time spent waiting for a DB connection, i.e. while being blocked on the `Datasource.getConnection()` call),[2] *with DB connection active* (the time spent working with the DB connection, i.e. between the return of the call `Datasource.getConnection()` and the call to `Connection.close()`),[3] and *with*

---

[2] The call to `Datasource.getConnection()` requests a DB connection from the pool, if one is not cached by the request.

[3] The call to `Connection.close()` is actually performed on a wrapper object, so it does not close the connection, but signals to the Database Connection Manager that the service request has finished working with the connection. The latter then is either kept cached for the request or returned to the pool (see Section 2.2.2 for details). We don't track database activities performed over database connections and the periods of "working with a DB connection" are demarcated by the calls to `Datasource.getConnection()` (start) and `Connection.close()` (end).

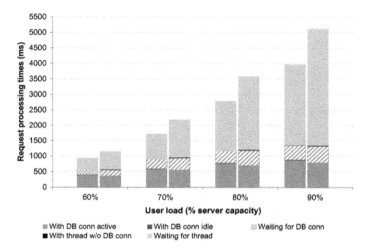

Figure 5.4: Breakdown of request processing time for the Buy Request request (left col.: request-wide DB connection caching, right col.: transaction-wide caching).

DB connection idle (the time spent processing the request with an idle DB connection cached).[4] Note that in the case of request-wide DB connection caching, *waiting for thread* corresponds to w_l^{THR}, *with thread w/o DB connection* — to p_i, *waiting for DB connection* — to w_l^{DB}, and *with DB connection active* and *with DB connection idle*, combined, constitute q_l.

To better understand the relative performance of the two connection caching methods, it is important to know how many times a DB connection is requested from the pool, for different request types. During the execution of the Search request a DB connection is requested from the pool 101 times (one time for the SQL query that returns IDs of certain 50 items,

---

[4] That is, when the connection is cached for the request between the call to `Connection.close()` and the next call to `Datasource.getConnection()` or the end of request execution.

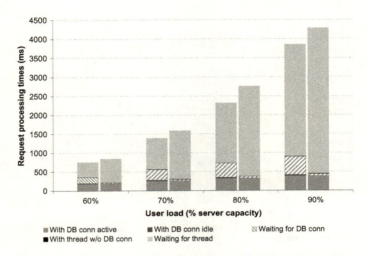

- With DB conn active　　■ With DB conn idle　　⊠ Waiting for DB conn
- With thread w/o DB conn　■ Waiting for thread

Figure 5.5: Breakdown of request processing time for the Buy Confirm request (left col.: request-wide DB connection caching, right col.: transaction-wide caching).

and 2 times for an EJB method invocation on each of the 50 Entity Beans, see explanation in Section 5.3). Buy Request results in 10 requests for a DB connection, and Buy Confirm incurs 1 request for a DB connection, because this service request is transactional, and the obtained DB connection is cached even in the default transaction-wide DB connection caching mechanism.

The first thing to notice is that *with DB connection idle* times are very small and are negligible compared with *with DB connection active* times (they aren't even seen on some charts). This means that request-wide DB connection caching does not waste much DB connection resources. Individual times of waiting for DB connection are larger in request-wide connection caching (than in transaction-wide connection caching), but this effect is compensated by the fact that a service request has only to endure one such waiting time period. Request-wide connection caching is beneficial for service requests that obtain (and return) DB connection from the pool many times — compare *waiting for DB connection* times for the Search and Buy Confirm service requests, which obtain DB connection from the pool 101 times and 1 time, respectively. The time to process a request after it was assigned to a thread, for the Search request, is significantly larger in default transaction-wide connection caching, because of the aforementioned effect. Given that Search requests constitute a large portion of user load that we used (namely, 32%), the average time requests (of all types) spend with a thread assigned is larger and, as a consequence, *waiting for thread* times are larger for *all* request types. This results in larger overall request processing times for *all* request types, in transaction-wide connection caching, compared with request-wide DB connection caching.

The main conclusion that we can draw by analyzing the relative performance of both connection caching methods, is that request-wide DB connection caching is beneficial in situations where a large portion of service requests is comprised of non-transactional requests implemented in a way that DB connections are requested from the pool many times per single service request execution. This characteristic is typical of the applications and workloads we target in this work.

5.5.3 Evaluation of the method for computing the optimal resource pool sizes

We evaluate the proposed method for computing the optimal number of server threads and DB connections on the TPC-W application, which is configured as described in Section 5.5.1.

In step 1, the values of p_i and q_i are gathered through the request execution profiling support using the user load parameters shown in Table 5.2 ("Profiling load" column). We use the following data points: all pairs (M, N), where $M = 5, 10, 15, 20, 30, 50$, $N = 1, 2, 4, 5, 10, 15, 20, 30, 40$, and $M \geq N$. Reasonable application performance was achieved with $5 \leq M \leq 30$, so we concentrate on this region. The server configuration used in the tests is the same as in the RDRP experiments (Section 4.6.1).

Table 5.2: Parameters of user loads used in the evaluation experiments (breakdown of load by request types (V_i) and average session length).

Request type	"Profiling load" (step 1)	"Load 1"	"Load 2"
Home	6.82%	5.53%	5.37%
Search	**31.93%**	**30.31%**	**48.07%**
Item	**42.73%**	**57.73%**	**41.55%**
Add To Cart	4.76%	1.76%	1.39%
Cart	2.03%	0.7%	0.53%
Register	3.58%	1.32%	1.03%
Buy Request	3.58%	1.32%	1.03%
Buy Confirm	3.58%	1.32%	1.03%
Total	100%	100%	100%
Average session length (number of requests)	14.67	18.07	18.62

In step 2, we interpolate functions $p_i(M,N)$ and $q_i(M,N)$ for the region $5 \leq M \leq 30$, $0 \leq N \leq M$. Figs. 5.6, 5.7, and 5.8 show examples of interpolated functions — $q_i(M,N)/N$ for the Search and Item requests, and function $p_i(M,N)$ for the Home request, respectively. Each curve on these charts corresponds to the function with fixed M (number of threads), $M = 5, \ldots, 30$, and is parameterized by N (number of DB connections).

The shapes of the function curves may be quite complex. They reflect the behavior of different request types, relative to the sizes of the thread and DB connection pools, and show how requests scale with increased number of threads and DB connections. Obviously, functions $p_i(M,N)$ and $q_i(M,N)$ depend on hardware, middleware, and database configurations. But most notably, we believe, they depend on the functionality and the implementation of the service requests, i.e., on the nature of the underlying work being done by the requests, on the way low-level resources (such as CPU, memory, IO) are used, and on the way concurrent requests interfere with each other (i.e., database locking and data contention issues). For example, the Search request, which performs complex read-only database queries, scales well and enjoys better performance with in-

128

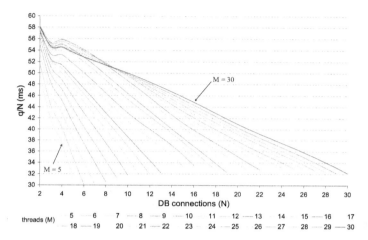

Figure 5.6: q_i for the Search request, divided by the number of DB connections.

creased degree of parallelism (Fig 5.6), while the Item request shows the best performance with relatively small number of threads and DB connections ($M, N = 5, \ldots, 8$, see Fig. 5.7).

In step 3 we get the values of maximum sustainable session throughput $\lambda(M, N)$, for every combination of M and N. We compute these values for the same load as we used in the "profiling tests" (Table 5.2). Fig. 5.9 shows function $\lambda(M, N)$, computed by our method.

We define $\lambda(N)$ as the maximum sustainable session throughput as a function of N, where M is chosen to achieve the best throughput for a given N:

$$\lambda(N) = \lambda(M_0, N) \mid M_0 = \underset{M}{\operatorname{argmax}} \lambda(M, N) \qquad (5.5)$$

Fig. 5.9 also shows $\lambda(N)$ computed by our method ("$\lambda(N)$ meth"), and obtained experimentally ("$\lambda(N)$ exp"). To obtain the latter, for each

129

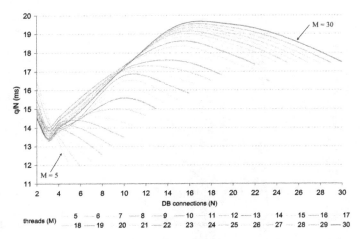

Figure 5.7: q_i for the Item request, divided by the number of DB connections.

optimal pair of (M_0, N) computed by the method (M_0 defined by equation (5.5)) we run tests with $(M_0 - 1, N)$, (M_0, N), $(M_0 + 1, N)$, and $(M_0 - 2, N)$, $(M_0 + 2, N)$ if needed, to determine the maximum session throughput in each case and confirm that M_0 is indeed the optimal for a given N.

As a matter of fact, it is difficult to tell the *exact* throughput of a server configuration due to non-determinism in its behavior, especially for user loads that we use (Poisson session arrivals, random inter-request times, see Section 3.1.4). One can tell only *approximate* request (session) throughput, which can be defined, for example, as the maximum λ, at which 60% of test runs complete with a request success rate of 100%. Therefore, the values of λ (session arrival rate) used in the tests determining the actual maximum session throughout are incremented with a granularity of 0.05 (e.g., 2.65, 2.70, 2.75, ...).

Our method succeeds in determining the value of M that achieves the

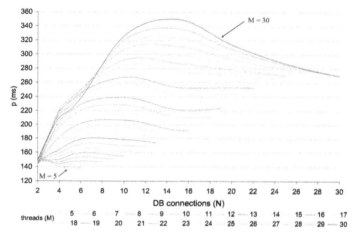

Figure 5.8: p_i for the Home request.

highest throughput for a given N (also referred to as "the optimal M for a given N"), and vice versa. However, it might not be exactly precise in determining the value of actual maximum session throughput, which may well happen to be a little lower than projected by the method. This effect can be attributed to the thread and DB connection "context switching"[5] and to the burstiness of the incoming user requests. However, the actual session throughput (determined by the experiments) always lies within a 5% error margin of the value predicted by the method.

It is interesting to notice that the optimal pairs of (M,N) are ones where N is very close to M, e.g., (8,6), (14,11), (30,26). This means that only a few additional threads are needed to do processing of requests that do not access the database. This is also seen in the fact that under load the

---

[5] A thread that releases a DB connection notifies the next waiting thread, and it may take some CPU cycles before the waiting thread grabs the released DB connection; in other words, a DB connection occurs to be occupied for a slightly greater time, than can be recorded.

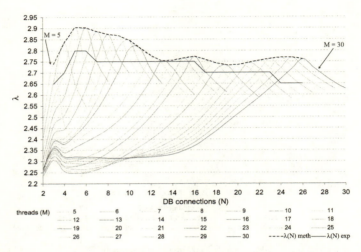

Figure 5.9: $\lambda(M,N)$ and $\lambda(N)$, computed by our method ("$\lambda(N)$ meth") and obtained experimentally ("$\lambda(N)$ exp"), for the "profiling load."

values of q_i's increase much higher than do the values of p_i's (Table 5.1). This indicates that requests, after being assigned to a server thread, spend a dominant portion of their processing time working with the DB connection.

In the next series of experiments we tested the ability of our method to work with user loads that differ from the one used in the "profiling tests." In preliminary tests we noticed that the dependence of p_i's and q_i's on the incoming request mix (V_i) is very weak, i.e., their values change insignificantly when the request load parameters V_i stay *close enough* to their initial values. This suggests that it might be possible to gather the values of p_i's and q_i's for some average (*representative*) user load, and later use them to compute the optimal number of threads and DB connections for loads that differ from the one used in the "profiling tests."

To verify this, we test our method on two user loads that differ from the

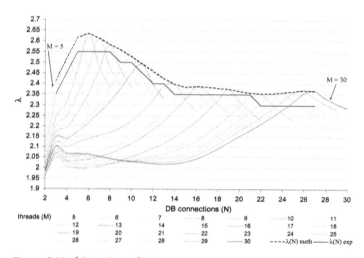

Figure 5.10: $\lambda(M,N)$ and $\lambda(N)$, computed by our method ("$\lambda(N)$ meth") and obtained experimentally ("$\lambda(N)$ exp"), for the "Load 1" user load.

"profiling load", but stay relatively *close* to it (with the values of V_i varying by no more than ± 15-20%). In computations, we use the same p_i's and q_i's obtained for the "profiling load". The parameters of these loads ("Load 1" and "Load 2") are shown in Table 5.2. As the "profiling load," these two loads are chosen to be representative of real-life shopping scenarios, where Search and Item requests dominate all other request types. The chosen loads represent the two extremes of the load spectrum — "Load 1" has a dominant portion of Item requests, while "Load 2" has a greater number of Search requests.

As with the "profiling load," we use our method to compute the values of $\lambda(M,N)$ and $\lambda(N)$, and perform a series of test runs to obtain the values of $\lambda(N)$ experimentally. Figs. 5.10 and 5.11 show the results of these computations and experiments for "Load 1" and "Load 2," respectively. As

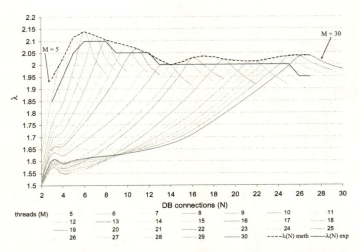

Figure 5.11: $\lambda(M,N)$ and $\lambda(N)$, computed by our method ("$\lambda(N)$ meth") and obtained experimentally ("$\lambda(N)$ exp"), for the "Load 2" user load.

we see, the method works well for both user loads. The method is able to compute the optimal number of threads and DB connections and the actual values of session throughput lie within a 5% margin of the values predicted by the method.

5.6 Chapter summary

In this chapter we presented the method that computes the optimal number of threads and database connections for a given application, its Web application server and database environment, and specific user load (request mix). The methodology is built on a model for request execution with 2-tier exclusive resource holding (1st tier — threads, 2nd tier — DB connections). This method uses information about *fine-grained server re-*

134

source utilization (Section 3.3), obtained through profiling of request execution in a limited set of off-line ("profiling") experiments, where the actual server environment is subjected to an artificial user load. Under real operating conditions, the method takes as input the *request flow* information (Section 3.1), obtained through on-line request profiling, and computes the maximum sustainable session throughput for a given number of threads and DB connections, and the mix of incoming user requests.

We evaluate the proposed methodology by testing it on the TPC-W application. The method is shown to be able to compute the values of the maximum sustained session throughput, which lie within a 5% error margin of the actual throughput achieved by the application under actual user load. Moreover, the method works for user loads, which differ from the load used in the "profiling tests," but are *close* to it. By being able to predict the session throughout for any input values of the number of threads and DB connections, the method gives a way to compute the number of threads and DB connections that maximize session throughput, thus enabling optimal utilization of these two pooled Web application server resources.

Chapter 6

Session Data Integrity

This chapter focuses on the problem of providing session data integrity guarantees, which was introduced earlier in Section 1.2.3. In Section 6.1 we formulate the problem and present our approach to solving it. Section 6.2 talks about the models used and the assumptions made, and among other issues introduces the three concurrency control algorithms for web sessions, which are used to provide session data integrity guarantees. In Section 6.3 we present our analytical models for concurrent web sessions with bounded inconsistency in shared data, which allow us to reason about various performance metrics achieved by the three algorithms. Section 6.4 describes our middleware infrastructure for data consistency enforcement and Section 6.5 presents our evaluation methodology and experimental results.

6.1 Problem formulation and our approach

As described earlier, the typical interaction of users with modern Internet services is organized into *sessions*. In the on-line shopping scenario for an e-Commerce web site introduced earlier, the multiple requests (1) search for particular products, (2) retrieve information about a specific item (e.g., quantity and price), (3) add it to the shopping cart, (4) initiate the check-out process, and (5) finally commit the order.

In scenarios of this kind, session requests can both *read* and *write* application data *shared* among several users of the service. Thus, execution of concurrent client sessions may affect each other by changing the shared application state. In the above example, the client's decision to commit the order (buying an item in step 5) is based on the information presented in step 2. Thus, if the quantity or price of the item has changed (as a result of concurrent client activities), it might be undesirable to allow the client to commit the order (step 5) based on incorrect information. At this point the service provider needs to make a decision of whether to proceed with the execution of the request: allowing the session with invalid data to progress can lead to potential financial penalties incurred by the service (e.g., selling an item which has become out of stock, or selling it at a lower price), while blocking the session's execution might result in user dissatisfaction and can lead to a drop in user loyalty. In the latter case the session execution is *deferred*, and handling of the case is relayed to customer service or awaits the intervention of system administrators, based on the nature of the business represented by the service.

A compromise would be to tolerate some *bounded degree* of *shared data inconsistency* [101, 145], denote it q (measured in some units, e.g., price or item quantity difference), which would allow more sessions to progress, while limiting the potential financial loss by the service. The current dominant approach in web-based shopping systems is to satisfy the client at all costs and never defer its session (which corresponds to tolerating $q = \infty$), but one could envision scenarios where imposing some limits on the tolerable session data inconsistency (and so — limiting the possible financial loss) at the expense of a small number of deferred sessions might be a more preferable alternative. Besides on-line shopping, examples of the systems where such tradeoffs might prove beneficial, are on-line trading systems and auctions.

To enforce that the chosen degree of data consistency is preserved, the service can rely on different *concurrency control* algorithms. Several such algorithms have been developed in the context of classical database transaction theory and for advanced transaction models (see Section 2.7). However, these algorithms need to be modified to be able to enforce session data consistency constraints, because of substantial differences between classical transactions and web sessions, which we discussed in Section 2.7.2.

In this work, we consider three concurrency control algorithms for web sessions — *Optimistic Validation*, *Locking*, and *Pessimistic Admission Control*. The algorithms work by *rejecting* the requests of the sessions for which they can not provide data consistency guarantees (so these sessions become *deferred*). However, they utilize different strategies in doing so, which leads to different number of deferred sessions, not known to the service provider in advance. In order to meaningfully trade off having to defer some sessions for guaranteed bounded session data inconsistency, the service provider can benefit from models that predict metrics such as the percentage of successfully completed sessions (as opposed to the percentage of deferred sessions), for certain degree of tolerable data inconsistency (the value of q), based on service particulars and information about how clients use the service.

To this end, we develop analytical models that characterize execution of concurrent web sessions with bounded shared data inconsistency, for each of the three discussed concurrency control algorithms. We present our models in the context of the sample *buyer* scenario for the TPC-W e-Commerce benchmark application (Section 2.4.1). We compare the results of our analytical models with the results of concurrent web session execution in a simulated, and in a real web application server environment.

Besides allowing one to quantitatively reason about tradeoffs between the benefits of limiting tolerable session data inconsistency and the drawbacks of necessarily deferring some sessions to enforce this data consistency, the models also permit comparison between concurrency control algorithms, with regards to the chosen metric of interest. In particular, since the proposed models use as input service usage parameters that are easily obtained through profiling of incoming client requests, one can build an *automated* decision making process as a part of the underlying middleware platform, that would choose an appropriate concurrency control algorithm in real time, in response to changing service usage patterns.

To test this claim we augment our middleware infrastructure implemented in the application server JBoss (Section 2.3) with the session data consistency enforcement capabilities and automated decision making func-

138

tionality described above. Session data consistency is enforced by the means of *intercepting* (and so — rejecting, if need be) service requests. The decision of which concurrency control method to use is made automatically, based on the analytical models and the parameters of service usage, obtained by the request profiling service.

6.2 Models and assumptions

The analytical models take as input information about user request flow structure, which comes in the form of the CBMG model (Section 3.1.2). We present the models in the context of the sample *buyer* scenario for the TPC-W transactional web e-Commerce benchmark application (Section 2.4.1), whose sessions adhere to the CBMG shown in Fig. 3.2. Each session starts with the Home request, and may end either after several Search and Item requests (we refer to such sessions as *browser* sessions), or after putting a (number of) item(s) in the shopping cart and completing the purchase (*buyer* session). To stress essential buyer activities in this sample scenario, we assume that once a user puts an item into the shopping cart, he never abandons the session and eventually commits the order. Each Item request carries an additional parameter — the `itemId` of the item to be displayed. We assume that there are S items in the store, and that the i-th item is picked with probability p_i^{item}. The Add To Cart request chooses the same item that was picked in the preceding Item request, and it puts it in the shopping cart with quantity 1.

As discussed in Section 3.1, we assume that new sessions arrive as a Poisson process [73] with arrival rate λ and that session inter-request times are independent with mean $1/\mu$, that is, requests from a session form a random process with the event arrival rate μ (see Section 3.1.4). When we state this explicitly, we assume a specific distribution of session inter-request times. We also discuss the affect of specific distributions of session inter-request times in Section 6.5.

When developing the models, we assume that a request is served immediately and is either admitted and processed by the service, or rejected, which in turn terminates that session. Request processing time, including serialization delays in the underlying database, is assumed to be negligible compared to the average session inter-request time. In Section 6.5 we discuss the motivation behind this assumption.

6.2.1 Session data consistency constraints

Information about the business-critical shared data that the service provider wants to cover by data consistency constraints can not be automatically extracted from the application structure or code — it needs to be identified by the service provider. To do this, we use the flexible application-generic OP-COP-VALP model for specification of conflicting operations and validation points, presented in Section 3.4.1. We will illustrate our analytical models for concurrent web sessions in the context of the following data consistency constraint specification for the TPC-W application:

> For each session, the quantity of an item (with id i) seen in the Buy Request state which presents an updated view of the shopping cart, can differ by no more than q_i units from the value seen by the Add To Cart request which inserted the item into the shopping cart. q_i may be different for different items in the store.

The mapping of this specification to the OP-COP-VALP model is the following (see also Fig. 6.1):

- OP is the Add To Cart request, with corr.Id being its itemId parameter; COP is the Buy Confirm request (which completes the purchase, records the order information, and decrements the items' quantities), with corr.Ids being the set of itemIds of the items in the shopping cart.

- NUM_VAL of the OP (Add To Cart) request is the available quantity of the item. The COP (Buy Confirm) request changes the correlated NUM_VAL value by decrementing it by the quantity of the item in the purchase (itemIds and quantities of the items in the purchase are

140

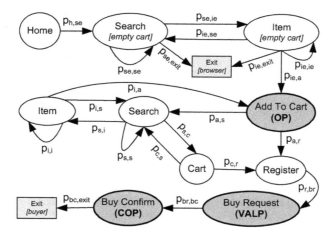

Figure 6.1: CBMG of a sample TPC-W buyer session with mappings of OP, COP, and VALP to the service requests.

all parameters of the Buy Confirm request). Thus, q is the relative inconsistency of NUM_VAL, that the service wishes to tolerate.

- Buy Request corresponds to a VALP which covers all OPs of the session.

6.2.2 Concurrency control algorithms

Concurrency control techniques in transaction processing theory can be classified into two categories: *locking* techniques and *validation* techniques. The spirit of the first is to *lock* shared resources, preventing concurrent processes from accessing a locked entity until a certain safe point of execution is reached (e.g., transaction *commit*). The approach in the second camp is to let concurrent processes execute in parallel, accessing shared resources, and to *validate* execution in the end, hoping that conflicts either did not happen or canceled each other out. Although these mechanisms are not

141

directly applicable to web sessions, one can come up with similar concurrency control algorithms for web sessions with data consistency constraints. The algorithms determine whether to allow execution of a request (with all possible effects on shared application state) or to reject it. Once a request from the session has been rejected, the whole session is deemed *deferred*, with no additional requests coming from that session. In this book, we work with the following three natural algorithms, which are based on the OP-COP-VALP model for specification of data consistency constraints:

- **Optimistic Validation**: admit all OP and COP requests; when a VALP request arrives, validate the OPs that it *covers* — and admit or reject the VALP request accordingly. This technique resembles *backward validation* of classical transactions.

- **No-Waiting Locking (Locking)**: this technique is applicable if every COP request in a session is preceded by a correlated OP request (think of OP and COP as READ and WRITE of the same data item). Assign a *logical lock* to each value of the corr.Id, and make the OP request obtain this lock when admitted and release the lock after the completion of the COP request. If OP can not obtain the lock it is immediately rejected (hence the name of the algorithm). Note that this technique has somewhat different semantics from the classical "no-waiting" locking — if the request is rejected the session is not restarted.

- **Pessimistic Admission Control**: admit OPs and VALPs; when a COP arrives, admit it only if it would not potentially invalidate OPs of other concurrent sessions. This technique resembles *forward validation* of classical transactions.

Note that these web session concurrency control algorithms build on top of serialization support of the underlying database and do not substitute conventional transactions — if the service logic requires it, the ACID properties of individual OP, COP, and VALP requests are guaranteed by the underlying middleware transaction service.

142

6.2.3 Metrics of interest

As client interaction with the service is organized in sessions and a client is satisfied only if its session successfully completes (i.e., it is not deferred), the measure of success of a particular concurrency control algorithm should be viewed in light of *how many sessions have completed successfully*. Therefore, we consider **percentage of successful sessions** as the main service performance metric throughout the chapter.

Another metric that we consider is the **percentage of requests belonging to successful sessions**, or simply **percentage of successful requests**, as a measure of what portion of system resources did good for clients, and what portion was wasted serving requests of deferred sessions. As we will see, the two metrics are not the same. While the first metric can be viewed as a *business* or *client satisfaction* metric, the second one is clearly a *system* metric.

Different concurrency control algorithms defer unsuccessful sessions at different stages of session execution, so the actual load on the service (e.g., request rate), produced by different algorithms is different. Therefore, another system metric we look at is the **effective request rate** seen by the service, measured in number of requests served per unit time (we count rejected requests too, because they also consume system resources).

6.3 Analytical models

In this section we present three analytical models, one for each concurrency control algorithm (Section 6.2.2). The models compute the three chosen metrics of interest (Section 6.2.3), based on the parameters of service usage. The models, although somewhat different, rely on the following three key modeling techniques, used in other modeling studies as well [127, 4, 129, 130]:

1. **Approximating independence assumptions.** Execution of multiple concurrent web sessions is a compound random process, comprised of multiple inter-dependent finite-living random processes representing each session, which are in turn spawned by the Poisson process of

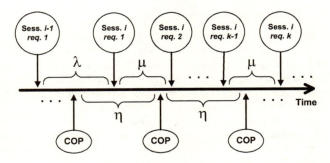

Figure 6.2: Analytical model.

new session arrivals. The inter-dependence is complicated further by
the presence of session data consistency constraints. To simplify analysis, we assume that certain events are *independent* and approximat-
able as a Poisson process. The main such assumption is that COP requests form a Poisson process (with arrival rate η) which is independent of the Poisson process of incoming new sessions (see Fig. 6.2).
Some of these assumptions are justified by the memorylessness property of Poisson process, in other cases they are not precisely correct,
because requests originate from slightly correlated processes. However, as our validation results in Section 6.5 show, these assumptions
prove a good approximation.

2. **Session enumeration technique.** In order to compute some proba-
bilistic parameters, when it is difficult to do so purely analytically, we
use the computational approach of *session enumeration*. We compute
the value of the desired parameter for a session that has a particular
known structure (sequence of requests). The final value of the parameter is the summation (over all possible sessions) of values obtained
for individual sessions, weighted by the probability of the session
having a specific structure. The number of possible session structures is, of course, infinite, but in the adopted CBMG session model,

144

the probability of a session having length greater than L_{max} decreases exponentially with growing L_{max}. For reasonably structured sessions with probabilities of transitions reflecting real-life service usage, it is sufficient to count all sessions of length less than 2 to 3 times the average session length (i.e., involving on the order of $30 - 40$ requests), to cover, say, 96-97% of all sessions, probability-wise. This makes it computationally feasible to implement the technique, which runs over the "majority" of session structures, and expect the running time of the modeling algorithm to be in the order of minutes, not hours. The enumeration algorithm also computes the probability space covered and specifically *adjusts* the computed value to *account for* sessions not enumerated.

3. **Fixed point iteration over an unknown value.** Due to the complex inter-dependent nature of concurrent session execution, it often happens that in order to compute a certain parameter P through the session enumeration technique, we need to know the value of some other parameter, say R, which in turn depends on P. To break this loop, we assume some value for P, use computation techniques to find R (and so P as well), and iterate the procedure until convergence to a fixed point.

Although we illustrate our models using the CBMG and associated data consistency constraints of our sample TPC-W buyer scenario (Fig. 3.2), we note that the approach itself is general enough to be tailored to other CBMGs and associated session data consistency constraints.

Recall that our TPC-W sessions are divided between *browser* and *buyer* sessions. A browser session becomes a buyer session when it moves from the Item [empty cart] state to the Add To Cart state (Fig. 3.2). The probability that a session eventually makes this transition (P_{buy}) is easily computable from the state transition probabilities $p_{i,j}$ (this apparatus was developed in the CBMG model [89]). This gives us the rate of incoming buyer sessions $\lambda_{buy} = \lambda P_{buy}$. The rest of the chapter will concentrate on the buyer sessions. To clarify the presentation, we use small letters to denote probability values that are given by the model, e.g., $p_{i,j}$, and capital letters to denote

Figure 6.3: Example of a TPC-W buyer session.

values that we introduce and that need to be computed, e.g., P_{buy}.

In our TPC-W buyer session, OPs are Add To Cart requests, each adding one item to the shopping cart with quantity 1. Recall that we have S items in the store, and probability of picking the i-th item is p_i^{item}. The corr.Id associated with each OP request is the itemId of the item put into the shopping cart. If a session has K OP requests (i.e., K items are put into the shopping cart, counting their quantities), we denote their corr.Ids (i.e., itemIds) as $i_1, i_2, \ldots, i_K$. Each OP request has an associated NUM_VAL value — the available quantity of the item at the moment of the request. Each individual COP with the same corr.Id i decreases this value by 1. The session is successful, if NUM_VAL decreases by no more than q_i, between the OP (Add To Cart) and the VALP (Buy Request) requests. A Buy Confirm request, if admitted, decrements the available quantities of items that were purchased. We view the Buy Confirm request as a *set of unit decrements*, as many of them for each itemId as was the quantity of the item in the purchase. With this notation, an admitted Buy Confirm request produces the set of individual COPs (K of them in total) with corr.Ids matching those of the OP requests in the session — $i_1, i_2, \ldots, i_K$. Throughout the rest of the chapter we will refer to the session in Fig. 6.3, as an example of a specific session structure. Note, that this session has two OPs with corr.Ids i_1 and i_2.

In all three analytical models, the first two percentage metrics — probability of session success (P) and percentage of requests belonging to successful sessions (REQ) — are computed by the session enumeration method, in which we actually enumerate not only session structures, but also all possible assignments of corr.Ids to OPs:

$$P = \sum_{\substack{\text{all sessions and} \\ \text{corr.Id assignments}}} P_{\text{sess}} \cdot P_{\text{succ}} \tag{6.1}$$

146

$$REQ = \frac{\sum_{\substack{\text{all sessions and} \\ \text{corr.Id assignments}}} P_{\text{sess}} \cdot P_{\text{succ}} \cdot L_{\text{succ}}}{L_{\text{av}}} \qquad (6.2)$$

P_{sess}, the probability of a session having a particular sequence of requests $k_1, k_2, \ldots, k_L$ and corr.Ids $i_1, i_2, \ldots, i_K$ assigned to its OPs is given by the formula:

$$P_{\text{sess}} = \prod_{j=1}^{L-1} p_{k_j, k_{j+1}} \cdot \prod_{j=1}^{K} p_{i_j}^{\text{item}} \qquad (6.3)$$

P_{succ} is the probability of a particular session completing successfully. L_{succ} is the number of requests in a particular session, when it is successful. L_{av} is the average number of requests in a session. The third metric — request rate (RATE) — is given by the formula:

$$RATE = \lambda \cdot L_{\text{av}} \qquad (6.4)$$

6.3.1 Optimistic Validation

The Optimistic Validation algorithm works by validating VALP requests (a single Buy Request in our case). The analytical model is built by assuming that we know the value of η — the arrival rate of COPs. Using the value of η we compute the probability of the Buy Request validation for a particular session structure. Using the session enumeration technique we compute the two percentage metrics (formulae (6.1) and (6.2)), along with η. Fixed point iteration over unknown η completes the process. In developing this model for Optimistic Validation we assume that session inter-request times are exponentially distributed (with parameter μ).

If a session is validated, its Buy Confirm request produces a set of K COPs. So the expression for η, used by the session enumeration technique, is:

$$\eta = \lambda_{\text{buy}} \sum_{\substack{\text{all sessions and} \\ \text{corr.Id assignments}}} P_{\text{sess}} \cdot P_{\text{succ}} \cdot K \qquad (6.5)$$

where the value of P_{sess} is given by (6.3). To compute P_{succ} — the probability of validating a session with a specific structure and a set of corr.Ids — we look at how many *distinct* corr.Ids are in the session (i.e., distinct

147

items are in the cart), based on the known values of $i_1, i_2, \ldots, i_K$. For each distinct corr.Id i, all OPs with this corr.Id are validated, if the corresponding NUM_VAL value (i.e., available quantity of the item) decreases by no more than q_i between the first OP (i.e., Add To Cart) and the VALP (i.e., Buy Request) requests. We assume, that validations of OPs with distinct corr.Ids are independent, so

$$P_{\text{succ}} = \prod_{\text{distinct } i \in \{i_1, i_2, \ldots, i_K\}} P_{\text{valid:corr.Id}=i},$$

where $P_{\text{valid:corr.Id}=i}$ — the probability of validating OP with corr.Id i, and with a specific distance between OP and VALP, which is inferred from the session structure. For example, in the session shown in Fig. 6.3 if the first item put into the cart has itemId 1 and the second has itemId 4, then the probability of session validation is the product of two validation probabilities: the first one — for OP with corr.Id 1 and a distance between OP and VALP of 5 requests, and the second — for OP with corr.Id 4 and a distance between OP and VALP of 2 requests.

We assume, that the portion of COPs with a particular corr.Id is proportional to the number of OPs with the same corr.Id, because if the session is validated, every OP is eventually followed by the COP with the same corr.Id. OP has corr.Id i with probability p_i^{item}. This means that the flow of COPs with a particular corr.Id i, if viewed as a Poisson process, has arrival rate $\eta_i = \eta \cdot p_i^{\text{item}}$. Thus, computation of $P_{\text{valid:corr.Id}=i}$ reduces to the following problem.

Given two Poisson processes, the first with arrival rate μ (session requests between OP and VALP), the other with arrival rate η_i (the flow of COPs with specific corr.Id i), find the probability that M requests from the first flow (M being the distance between OP and VALP, known from the session structure) come earlier than Q requests from the second flow (Q being actually $q_i + 1$, where q_i is the tolerable inconsistency, because the $q_i + 1$-st COP will invalidate OP). This probability (let's denote it $P_{\text{succ}}(\mu, M, \eta_i, Q)$) is exactly $P_{\text{valid:corr.Id}=i}$.

The probability that exactly k requests arrive in a Poisson process with arrival rate μ in the interval $(0,t)$: $P(\mu,k,t) = \frac{(\mu t)^k}{k!}e^{-\mu t}$. The PDF of the random variable representing the time of the M-th request arrival is

$$\text{pdf}_{\mu,M}(t) = \lim_{\Delta t \to 0} \frac{P\{M^{\text{th}}\text{ req. arr. in }(t,t+\Delta t)\}}{\Delta t} =$$

$$= \lim_{\Delta t \to 0} \frac{P(\mu,M-1,t)\cdot P(\mu,1,\Delta t)}{\Delta t} = \frac{(\mu t)^{M-1}\cdot \mu \cdot e^{-\mu t}}{(M-1)!}$$

$P_{\text{succ}}(\mu,M,\eta_i,Q)$ is obtained as the convolution of the PDF $\text{pdf}_{\mu,M}(t)$ of the time of the M-th request arrival in the first process and the probability that by that time there will be less than Q requests that would have arrived in the second Poisson process, $P(\eta_i,<Q,t)$. The latter is equal to $\sum_{k=0}^{Q-1} P(\eta_i,k,t) = \sum_{k=0}^{Q-1} \frac{(\eta_i t)^k}{k!}e^{-\eta_i t}$, and thus (we omit some details for brevity):

$$P_{\text{succ}}(\mu,M,\eta_i,Q) = \int_0^\infty P(\eta_i,<Q,t)\cdot \text{pdf}_{\mu,M}(t)dt =$$

$$= \int_0^\infty \left(\sum_{k=0}^{Q-1} \frac{(\eta_i t)^k}{k!}e^{-\eta_i t} \right) \frac{(\mu t)^{M-1}\cdot \mu \cdot e^{-\mu t}}{(M-1)!}dt = \dots$$

$$= \sum_{k=0}^{Q-1} \frac{\eta_i^k \cdot \mu^M}{k!\cdot(M-1)!\cdot(\mu+\eta_i)^{k+M}} \int_0^\infty t^{k+M-1}\cdot e^{-t}dt =$$

$$= \frac{\mu^M}{(M-1)!\cdot(\mu+\eta_i)^M} \sum_{k=0}^{Q-1} \frac{\eta_i^k}{k!\cdot(\mu+\eta_i)^k}\Gamma(k+M) \quad (6.6)$$

where $\Gamma(z) = \int_0^\infty t^{z-1}\cdot e^{-t}dt$ is the Gamma function [5], defined for complex values z, and known for positive integer k: $\Gamma(k) = (k-1)!$. Substituting this into equation (6.6) gives the final expression for $P_{\text{succ}}(\mu,M,\eta_i,Q)$:

$$\frac{\mu^M}{(M-1)!\cdot(\mu+\eta_i)^M} \sum_{k=0}^{Q-1} \frac{(k+M-1)!\cdot \eta_i^k}{k!\cdot(\mu+\eta_i)^k}$$

Finding P and REQ is completed by the fixed point iteration process over unknown η. The value given by r.h.s. of (6.5), if viewed as a function of η is a strictly decreasing function, because the greater the argument (the

149

assumed value of η), the fewer the number of validated sessions, and, in turn, the less the value of the r.h.s. of (6.5). Finding the intersection of a strictly decreasing positive function with the function $y = x$ is straightforward.

To compute effective request rate (RATE) by formula (6.4), we need to know L_{av}. If sessions are allowed to progress till the end, then the average session length (L_{av}^{ideal}) can be easily computed from the CBMG state transition probabilities $p_{i,j}$ (see Section 3.1.4, formulae (3.1) and (3.2)). The presence of the concurrency control algorithm makes some sessions shorter, because they are rejected. Identifying the points in a session's structure when the session can be rejected and comparing its length with the length of the same session running in the absence of any concurrency control algorithms, shows how L_{av} relates to L_{av}^{ideal}. In the case of Optimistic Validation method and the particular CBMG of the TPC-W session we consider, we conclude that every unsuccessful session is one request shorter than when it is successful, because the Buy Request is rejected and there is no final Buy Confirm request. Therefore, $L_{av} = L_{av}^{ideal} + P - 1$.

The complexity of the algorithm is linear in q_i, polynomial in S and the number of states in the CBMG, and exponential in L_{max} (the maximum length of sessions counted in the session enumeration technique). The latter parameter contributes the most to the complexity of the computation, but as we pointed out earlier (during the discussion of the session enumeration technique), being on the order of several dozens for reasonably structured real-life sessions, it makes it computationally feasible to use the algorithm.

6.3.2 Locking

Recall, that the Locking algorithm works by assigning $q_i + 1$ *logical locks* to each corr.Id value i, where q_i is the tolerable NUM_VAL inconsistency. Each OP tries to obtain a lock associated with the OP's corr.Id. If it does not succeed, the request is rejected, the session is considered aborted, and the locks held by the session are released. All locks are released after the COP request.

In the model for the Locking algorithm we assume that we know the values of P_{lock} — the probability that OP (regardless of its corr.Id) suc-

150

ceeds in obtaining a lock and T — the average time the lock is held for. P_{lock} is then used to compute λ_{OP} — the arrival rate of OPs. All three values are used to compute the probability of a particular session's success (P_{succ}), which is used by the session enumeration technique to compute all three metrics of interest (formulae (6.1), (6.2) and (6.4)), along with the values of P_{lock} and T. Fixed point iteration over unknown P_{lock} and T completes the model.

A session is successful if it acquires the lock on every OP request, so

$$P_{succ} = \prod_{j=1}^{K} P_{lock:i_j} \qquad (6.7)$$

where $P_{lock:i}$ is the probability of obtaining the lock for corr.Id i (we assume that the probabilities of obtaining locks for different corr.Ids are independent).

Finding $P_{lock:i}$ is the cornerstone of the model. To achieve this, we need λ_{OP} — the arrival rate of OP requests. Using the probabilities of state transitions $p_{i,j}$ it is easy to compute P_{ret} — the probability that after visiting the Add To Cart state a session will return to it again (see [89]). In the Locking algorithm, the progress of a *buyer* session is conditional on it being admitted in every Add To Cart request, so the probability of returning to the Add To Cart state is equal to $P_{lock}P_{ret}$. In addition to the first OP request in each buyer session, which contributes an arrival rate portion of λ_{buy} towards λ_{OP}, there is the flow of second OPs with arrival rate $\lambda_{buy}P_{lock}P_{ret}$, the flow of third OPs with arrival rate $\lambda_{buy}(P_{lock}P_{ret})^2$, and so on. Therefore,

$$\lambda_{OP} = \lambda_{buy} \sum_{k=0}^{\infty} (P_{lock}P_{ret})^k = \frac{\lambda_{buy}}{1 - P_{lock}P_{ret}} \qquad (6.8)$$

The overall flow of OPs divides into S subflows of requests with a particular corr.Id i, with arrival rates $\lambda_{OP} \cdot p_i^{item}$. For each corr.Id i, we consider OP requests as "customers", $q_i + 1$ locks as $q_i + 1$ "servers" and the time between an OP request and the corresponding COP request (during which the lock is held) in a session as "customer service time". Then the $q_i + 1$-lock algorithm of the Locking method introduces the virtual queueing system **M/G/q_i+1/q_i+1** [60], with the arrival rate of "customers" being

$\lambda_{OP} \cdot p_i^{\text{item}}$. The number of "customers" in such a system in the steady state — random variable ξ — depends only on the expected value of the distribution G (which represents "customer service time"), i.e., only on the average time of holding a lock — T. It is possible to obtain the lock only if the corresponding queueing system is not full, i.e., there are fewer than $q_i + 1$ "customers" in the system, therefore,

$$P_{\text{lock}:i} = \text{pr}(\xi < q_i + 1) = 1 - \frac{\frac{(\lambda_{OP} \cdot p_i^{\text{item}} \cdot T)^{q_i+1}}{(q_i+1)!}}{\sum_{k=0}^{q_i+1} \frac{(\lambda_{OP} \cdot p_i^{\text{item}} \cdot T)^k}{k!}} \tag{6.9}$$

Imagine that we know the values of P_{lock} and T. Equation (6.8) gives us the value of λ_{OP}. Then, in the session enumeration phase we compute the metrics of interest, using (6.7) and (6.9). The value of P_{lock} is computed by observing that $P_{\text{lock}} = \sum_{i=1}^{S} p_i^{\text{item}} \cdot P_{\text{lock}:i}$.

T is also computed by the session enumeration technique:

$$T = \sum_{\substack{\text{all sessions and} \\ \text{corr.Id assignments}}} P_{\text{sess}} \cdot T_{\text{sess}},$$

where T_{sess} is the average time a lock is held in a particular session. The value of P_{sess}, the probability of a session having a particular structure and a particular corr.Id assignments to its OPs, is given by (6.3). In the M/G/c/c system, customer service time is counted only for the customers *admitted* to the system. The zero time of a customer discarded without serving due to the limited server capacity does not count towards average customer service time. Therefore, in the computation of T_{sess}, we count only non-zero locking time periods, and among all $K + 1$ possible lock acquisition outcomes we consider only the K outcomes *that start with the first* OP *having obtained its lock*. For each outcome, we know the position of its OP — COP periods (when the locks are acquired and released) and their average duration. For example, if both OPs obtain locks in the example in Fig. 6.3, then we have two locking periods, the first lasting for $6/\mu$, on average, the second for $3/\mu$, with the average of $4.5/\mu$ for this outcome ($1/\mu$ is the average session inter-request time). If the second OP fails in obtaining the lock, we end up having only one locking period (between the first and the second OPs) lasting for $3/\mu$, on average. So for the session example in Fig. 6.3 we have: $T_{\text{sess}} = P_{\text{lock}:i_2}(4.5/\mu) + (1 - P_{\text{lock}:i_2})(3/\mu)$.

The average number of requests in a session (L_{av}), used to compute REQ in (6.2) and RATE in (6.4), is also computed using the session enumeration technique in a manner analogous to computing T_{sess} — for each possible lock acquisition outcome we know the number of requests in the session.

The Locking algorithm model is completed by fixed point iteration over the pair of unknown (P_{lock},T). Specifically, we start by assigning P_{lock} any value, say 0.5, and T — its lower bound, the average value of just one inter-request time period ($1/\mu$), and compute new values of P_{lock} and T by session enumeration. These new values serve as input for the next iteration, and the process repeats. Our experiments show that this process converges very quickly to the fixed point. The complexity of the whole algorithm is analogous to that of the Optimistic Validation algorithm.

6.3.3 Pessimistic Admission Control

This algorithm gives the worst performance with regards to the metrics of interest (we defer discussion of the reasons to Section 6.5), so models for it are irrelevant if one's goal is to maximize the metrics. We present it in this book only for completeness, restricting our attention to only the strict consistency case — $q = 0$. Recall, that the Pessimistic Admission Control algorithm works by admitting the COP requests that are not going to potentially invalidate other sessions.

Unlike the first two models, the model for the Pessimistic Admission Control algorithm does not require a fixed point iteration. First, we compute T — the average time between an OP and a VALP requests in a session. This value is used in the session enumeration to compute P_{succ} for a particular session, to get the first two metrics — P and REQ (formulae (6.1) and (6.2)). For the particular CBMG of the TPC-W session we consider, the number of requests in a session does not depend on its success, because possible request rejection only happens in the last request of the session — the Buy Confirm request. Therefore, the average session length (L_{av}) is the same as in the absence of any concurrency control algorithms — $L_{\text{av}}^{\text{ideal}}$, which is computed from $p_{i,j}$ (see [89]). This observation completes the

153

model by computing the RATE metric (equation (6.4)). The complexity of the whole algorithm is analogous to that of the Optimistic Validation algorithm.

We compute T, the average time between an OP and the VALP requests in a session, in a separate session enumeration pass. The value of T for a particular session is immediately seen from the session's structure. For the session in Fig. 6.3, it is equal to $3.5/\mu$, because there are two OP — VALP periods, of 5 and 2 inter-request times, respectively. Note that in general, T depends solely on the structure of CBMG and its state transition probabilities $p_{i,j}$.

In the TPC-W buyer session, the COP (i.e., Buy Confirm) request is admitted, if all individual COPs, comprising it, are admitted. In the strict consistency case ($q = 0$), if an individual COP performing a unit decrement of NUM_VAL for a particular corr.Id is admitted from a session, this implies that no concurrently active sessions involve that corr.Id. Therefore, an arbitrary number of additional COPs for the same corr.Id from the same session can also be admitted at the same time. Therefore,

$$P_{\text{succ}} = \prod_{\text{distinct } j \in \{i_1, i_2, \dots, i_K\}} P_{\text{admit}:j}$$

where $P_{\text{admit}:j}$ is the probability that COP with corr.Id j is admitted (we assume independence for different corr.Ids).

To compute $P_{\text{admit}:j}$, we need to know λ_{OP} — the arrival rate of OP requests. Each session produces, on average, V_{add} number of OP requests, where V_{add} is the average number of visits to the Add To Cart state (easily computable from $p_{i,j}$ [89]). Therefore, $\lambda_{\text{OP}} = \lambda_{\text{buy}} V_{\text{add}}$. The arrival rate of OPs with corr.Id i is $\lambda_{\text{OP}} \cdot p_i^{\text{item}}$. For each corr.Id i, we consider the following virtual queueing system: OP requests are "customers", the "customers" are "served" while the session is between the OP and the VALP requests. There are an infinite number of "servers" in the system, because all sessions are allowed to progress between an OP and the VALP. The queueing system described is **M/G/∞** [60] with the arrival rate of customers being $\lambda_{\text{OP}} \cdot p_i^{\text{item}}$. The number of customers in the system in the steady state is a random variable (denoted by ξ_i for corr.Id i). An individual COP with corr.Id i is admitted if there are no concurrently active sessions that involve the same `corr.Id` i, i.e., $\xi_i = 0$. Therefore,

$$P_{\mathrm{admit}:i} = \mathrm{pr}(\xi_i = 0) = \frac{(\lambda_{\mathrm{OP}} \cdot p_i^{\mathrm{item}} \cdot T)^k}{k!} e^{-\lambda_{\mathrm{OP}} \cdot p_i^{\mathrm{item}} \cdot T}$$

where T is the expected value of distribution G (representing customer service time), i.e., the average time between an OP and a VALP requests in a session, which was computed earlier.

6.4 Middleware infrastructure for data consistency enforcement

The middleware mechanisms enforce session data consistency constraints working only at the level of the abstract OP-COP-VALP model, with mapping of service requests to OPs, COPs and VALPs, and other information specified by the service provider. The benefits of this approach are that (1) the application code does not contain any concurrency control functionality and does not need to be changed to allow data consistency enforcement, and (2) this approach permits dynamic adaptation of concurrency control policies to changes in parameters of service usage, in order to maximize the metric of interest.

We augmented the middleware infrastructure that we implemented in the application server JBoss (Section 2.3) with the dynamic web session concurrency control capabilities described above. Session data consistency is enforced by the means of *intercepting* (and so — rejecting, if need be) service requests. This interception and interpretation of service requests is done at the EJB tier level, i.e. at the level of invocations to middle tier components (Section 2.2.1), rather that at the web tier level, i.e. at the level of HTTP requests. Recall, that concurrency control algorithms may require the knowledge of a request's parameters and its return value, in order to correlate the request and to compute the *Numerical Distance* in the OP-COP-VALP model (Section 3.4.1). At the web tier level, a request's parameters are encoded in the request's URL, and the request return value is the whole HTML page, while at the EJB tier level they are represented by convenient Java objects.

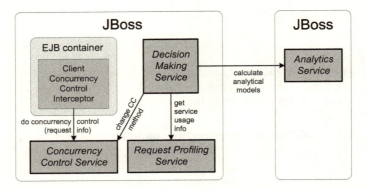

Figure 6.4: Middleware infrastructure for web session data consistency enforcement.

There are several reasons for choosing the EJB tier to intercept client requests. First, objects facilitate simple and type-safe extraction and manipulation of the application data, as opposed to cumbersome and error-prone parsing of URLs and HTTP pages. Second, the URL of the request may not provide sufficient information to identify what happened with the application state: for example, the URL of the TPC-W Buy Confirm request (http://host_name/tpcw/buy_confirm) does not contain any information about which items were bought — this information is stored in the session state and is revealed at the EJB tier level, when corresponding EJB components are invoked, as a part of the request execution.

The interception of user requests at the EJB tier level is enabled by the JBoss' EJB invocation model (Section 2.3.2), which allows insertion of additional *client-side* and *server-side* request interceptors in order to control the flow of request execution (e.g., to reject a method invocation). We add a client-side interceptor *Client Concurrency Control Interceptor*, which intercepts user requests, based on the predefined mapping of EJB invocations to OPs, COPs and VALPs. Fig. 6.4 shows the structural organization of our concurrency control infrastructure, which consists of the following submodules, each of which is implemented as a JMX MBean (Section 2.3.1) in order to standardize access to it and facilitate inter-module communication.

Request Profiling Service. Performs automatic real-time monitoring of client requests to extract parameters of service usage and to maintain the histories of session requests (Section 3.5.1). Produces estimates on the service usage parameters (i.e., λ, μ, p_i^{item}, and the CBMG state transition probabilities $p_{i,j}$), based on the observed history of client requests. The produced parameter estimates are accompanied with the 95% confidence intervals (see details in Section 3.5.2).

Concurrency Control Service. Performs actual concurrency control for web sessions according to the employed algorithm, by rejecting appropriate client requests, which are intercepted by the EJB *Client Concurrency Control Interceptor*. The algorithms are tailored to be able to switch concurrency control methods on the fly and still enforce data consistency for older sessions that started before the switch.

Analytics Service. Computes the analytical models, for a given input of model parameters: S, q_i (specified by the service provider) and λ, μ, p_i^{item}, and the CBMG state transition probabilities $p_{i,j}$ (obtained by the Request Profiling Service). This service runs on a separate application server because of its CPU intensive nature.

Decision Making Service. This is the main control module that orchestrates actions of the other infrastructure services. It periodically extracts the model parameters from the Request Profiling Service, computes the models using the Analytics Service and decides to switch to the better concurrency control algorithm if that shows metric benefits greater than a predefined threshold. Care is taken to avoid switching the algorithm due to a transient fluctuation in service usage (Section 3.5.2).

157

6.5 Experimental evaluation

First, we validate that our analytical models produce results that match the metric values obtained in a real world concurrent execution of web sessions. Second, we evaluate the behavior of and the benefits from dynamic adaptation of concurrency control algorithms.

6.5.1 Model validation

To validate our models we conducted the following two sets of experiments:

1. Execute concurrent TPC-W sessions with bounded data inconsistency in a simulation environment, implemented in Java and consisting of a virtual server with a logical rendering of TPC-W (with no actual database accesses) and a driver to simulate client load. This simulation represents an ideal rendering of the process, with resource contention limited only to Java synchronization, and request response times being effectively zero.

2. Run concurrent sessions against the TPC-W application deployed in a real web server environment. For these tests, we used the following TPC-W configuration values: NUM_ITEMS = 1000, NUM_EBS = 10 (Section 2.4.1). The server testbed configuration was the same as in the RDRP experiments (Fig. 4.5). The maximum sustainable request rate of the web application server was approximately 40 req/s.[1]

The parameter space of the sample TPC-W buyer CBMG with the specified data consistency constraints is very large — it consists of $p_{i,j}$ (state transition probabilities), S (number of items in the on-line store), p_i^{item} (probability of picking the i-th item), λ, μ (client load parameters), and q_i (tolerable consistency). We conducted the experiments for several sets of values, varying parameters in all dimensions of this space. All of them

---

[1] This seemingly low server throughput is attributed, first, to the underprovisioned one generation old machines we were using for the experiments, and second, to the fact that we did not perform scrutinized database and TPC-W application tuning. Unlike in typical TPC-W usage, the purpose of the tests was not to stress the database, but rather to exercise data conflicts among different web sessions

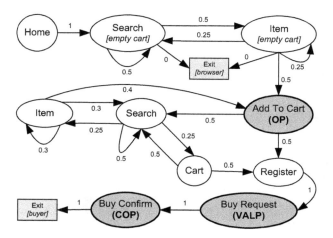

Figure 6.5: CBMG of the TPC-W buyer session used in the experiments validating analytical models.

showed that the analytical models produce results closely corresponding to those of the simulation and the real web server environment experiments. We will show and discuss the results of experiments for a "typical" on-line store workload, in which we fix all parameters except λ, which varies to present different client load, and q_i, for which we report on three sets of experiments: the strict consistency case ($q_i = 0$, for all items) and two relaxed consistency ones ($q_i = 6$ and $q_i = 30$).

As we discussed in Section 2.5.1, session inter-request (user think) times for e-Commerce web sites are reported to have either an exponential or a log-normal distribution. In most of our experiments we use exponentially distributed session inter-request times. Later in the section we study how our results would differ if session inter-request times instead followed a log-normal distribution. The values of CBMG state transition probabilities $p_{i,j}$ for the chosen web workload are shown in Fig. 6.5 – note that the

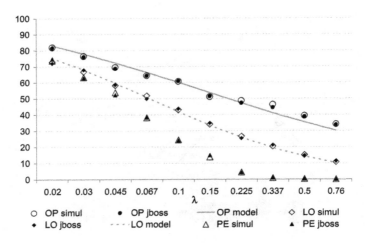

Figure 6.6: Percentage of successful sessions, for $q = 0$.

given CBMG has only buyer sessions. The other parameters are: $S = 5$;[2] $p_i^{item} = 0.2$ for $i = 1 \ldots 5$; $\mu = 0.1$, (it corresponds to an average session inter-request time of 10s). We have assumed for our models that request *processing* times are negligible compared to session *inter-request* times. This assumption is based on the fact that user *think* time is generally much higher (in order of tens of seconds) than users are willing to wait for request response (several seconds). In our JBoss/MySQL tests, request response times were generally in the 20-100ms span, reaching 350ms under the maximum load (compare it to 10s of average session inter-request time).

Figs. 6.6, 6.7, 6.8, and 6.9 compare the results of the two main metrics — the percentage of successful sessions and the percentage of requests belonging to successful sessions — for the three algorithms — Optimistic Validation (OP), Locking (LO), and Pessimistic Admission Control (PE),

---

[2] Having $S = 5$ does not mean that the store has only 5 items. A model's items may correspond to only those specific *hot-spot* items, for which the service provider wants to guarantee bounded data inconsistency.

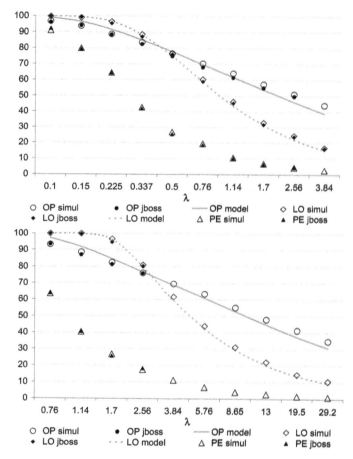

Figure 6.7: Percentage of successful sessions, for $q = 6$ (above) and $q = 30$ (below).

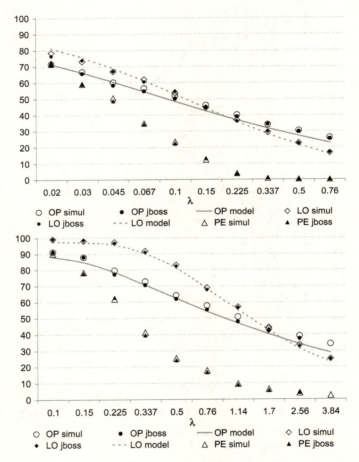

Figure 6.8: Percentage of requests belonging to successful sessions, for $q = 0$ (above) and $q = 6$ (below).

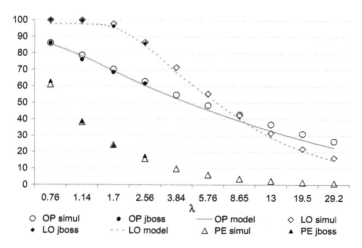

Figure 6.9: Percentage of requests belonging to successful sessions, for $q = 30$.

obtained in the simulation experiments (simul), in the JBoss/MySQL web server tests (jboss), and by the analytical models (model). We do not include in the charts the analytical model results for Pessimistic Admission Control, because it is always outperformed by the other two algorithms. The charts are also missing the JBoss test results for λ greater than 2.56, which we were unable to run due to limited server capacity.

The first observation is that the results of the models closely match both the simulation and the real web server environment results, which validates our proposed models. The models do sometimes have a little discrepancy with the experimental results, which tends to grow towards the ends of the λ/μ spectrum (note that λ/μ determines the "conflict rate" — the greater the value, the greater the number of concurrent sessions running, the more data conflicts they see, the less the values of the two percentage metrics of interest). However, it often happens that at the ends of the spectrum we have a clear algorithm winner, so discrepancy between the model and mea-

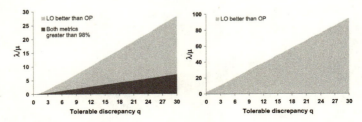

Figure 6.10: Algorithm performance comparison for the percentage of successful sessions (left) and the percentage of requests belonging to successful sessions (right).

surements does not hamper choosing the best concurrency control method. For example, with a large conflict rate (at the right end of the spectrum), Optimistic Validation always performs better than the other two algorithms.

Pessimistic Admission Control. This algorithm always performs worse than the other two, with respect to both percentage metrics. This happens, to our understanding, because of the "altruistic" nature of the method — sessions are rejected on COPs to give way to concurrent ones which otherwise would have been invalidated, but some of those sessions will also end up getting rejected, so some sessions are sacrificed in vain.

Optimistic Validation vs. Locking. These two methods compete to achieve the best value for the metrics. Optimistic Validation's "selfish" approach seems to work better for higher rates of conflicts. The Locking algorithm is more "thoughtful" in that it works by rejecting sessions earlier (on OP requests), when it just sees the possibility of later conflicts. It may reject some sessions prematurely, but it lets other sessions run in a less competitive environment. And it seems to work, especially for higher values of q_i, where for lower rates of conflicts the Locking method outperforms its rival in both percentage metrics. The algorithm also works better for the percentage of successful requests metric, than it does for the percentage of successful sessions. The reason for this lies in the nature of the algorithm

164

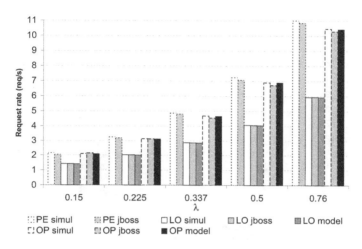

Figure 6.11: Request rate for $q = 0$.

— it rejects unsuccessful sessions earlier in their lifetime, which makes them considerably shorter than successful ones. This, in turn, increases the portion of requests that belong to successful sessions.

To summarize the differences in performance of the Optimistic Validation and the Locking algorithms, we identify the regions where one algorithm works better than the other, according to the analytical models. Note that in the ideal setting, the "rate of conflicts" (and so — both of the metrics) depend only on the ratio of λ and μ. As in the previous experiments, we fixed the values of all the parameters except λ, μ and q_i. Gray areas in Fig. 6.10 show the regions where the Locking algorithm outperforms the Optimistic Validation, for the percentage of successful sessions (left chart), and the percentage of requests belonging to successful sessions (right chart). In both charts, the X axis plots the value of tolerable inconsistency q_i (equal for all items), from 0 to 30, and the Y axis plots the ratio λ/μ. We only considered the cases where at least one of the metrics lies

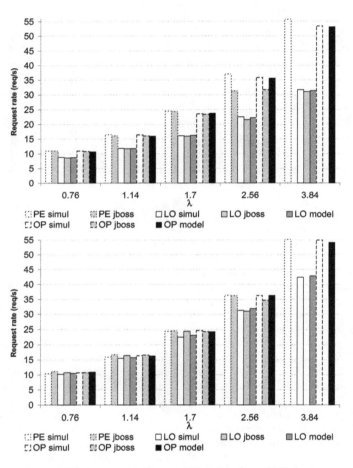

Figure 6.12: Request rate for $q = 6$ (above) and $q = 30$ (below).

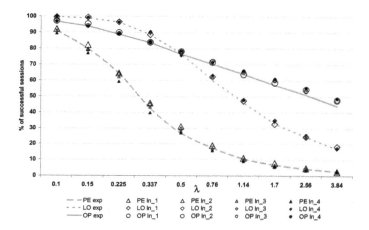

Figure 6.13: Percentage of successful sessions, for the four log-normal and one exponential distribution of session inter-request times ($q_i = 6$).

in the interval of 2% – 98%. The dark gray area in the left chart shows the region where the metrics for both algorithms are greater than 98%.

Effective request rate. Fig. 6.11 and 6.12 show the results for the third metric of interest — effective request rate. Note that for greater values of λ, request rates of the web server experiments are a little bit lower than the predicted and the simulation ones. This happens because under normal load, request response times are in the order of 20–100ms span, which is indeed negligible compared to the session inter-request times (10s on average). However, under higher load, response times become higher (and reach 300–350ms for $\lambda = 2.56$). These increased response times start making a slightly noticeable contribution to the interval between *sending* the requests, which become higher, so the effective request rate decreases.

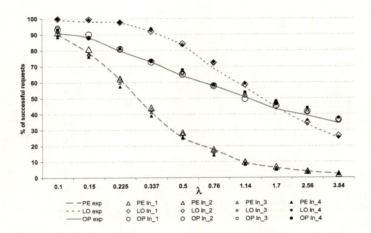

Figure 6.14: Percentage of requests belonging to successful sessions, for the four log-normal and one exponential distribution of session inter-request times ($q_i = 6$).

Server capacity considerations. Operating under higher user loads also reveals another major difference between the Optimistic Validation and the Locking algorithms — the Locking method produces lower request rates on the service. This happens because of the shorter sessions in the Locking algorithm, which stems from the algorithm's main policy — stop executing potential unsuccessful sessions earlier. This difference may become important if the service operates under server capacity limitations — the algorithm may become preferable over the Optimistic Validation technique, as one producing lesser load on the service, or with request rates better matching prescribed quotas. For example, we generally were unable to conduct experiments with λ being 3.84 and higher, because the projected request rates surpassed the capability of our web application server environment (~ 40 req/s).

Table 6.1: The client load of the dynamic adaptation experiments.

Phase	Phase 1	Phase 2	Phase 3	Phase 4	Phase 5
Model parameters	Buyer-1, $S=5$, $p_i^{item}=0.2$, $\lambda=3$, $q_i=10$	Buyer-1, $S=5$, $p_i^{item}=0.2$, $\lambda=1$, $q_i=10$	**Buyer-2**, $S=5$, $p_i^{item}=0.2$, $\lambda=0.5$, $q_i=10$	Buyer-2, $S=5$, $p_i^{item}=0.2$, $\lambda=0.5$, $q_i=3$	Buyer-2, $S=5$, $p_i^{item}=\{0.8,0.1,0.04, 0.03,0.03\}$, $\lambda=0.5$, $q_i=3$

Log-normal distribution of session inter-request times. By default, we used exponentially distributed session inter-request times in our experiments, but as we discussed in Section 2.5.1, some analyses of web traces shows that they actually might resemble more a log-normal distribution. To find out how the metrics of interest depend on the session inter-request times, we conducted additional simulations with four different log-normal distributions used as the session inter-request times: Ln(2.12;0.6), Ln(2.12;0.6), Ln(1.8;1), and Ln(1.58;1.2), chosen so that their mean values were 10s, matching that of the exponential distribution Exp(0.1) used in the previous simulations (see Section 3.1.4 for additional details). Fig. 6.13 and 6.14 show the two main percentage metrics, for the case of $q_i=6$. As we can see, the metrics are quite insensitive to the actual distribution of session inter-request times (but rather depend on its mean value), as was also suggested by our analytical models; only the model for Optimistic Validation used a specific distribution of session inter-request times.

6.5.2 Dynamic adaptation of concurrency control algorithms

To evaluate the behavior and the benefits of the dynamic adaptation of concurrency control algorithms, we conducted three experiments with our infrastructure. The first two fixed the concurrency control algorithm (Optimistic Validation and Locking), and the third tested automatic adaptation, with the objective of maximizing the percentage of successful sessions. All three experiments used the same client load and service-specific parameters, which consisted of the 5 phases shown in Table 6.1 (the two CBMGs used for the client load — "Buyer-1" and "Buyer-2" — are shown in

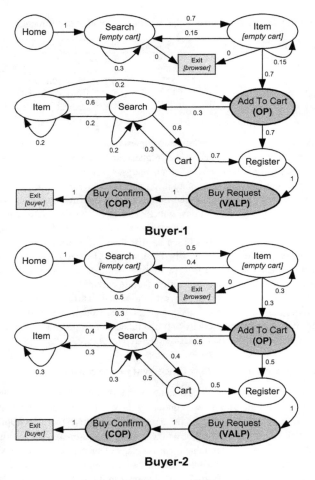

Figure 6.15: The CBMGs used in the dynamic adaptation experiments.

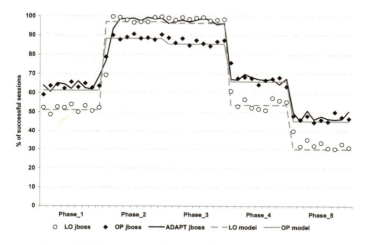

Figure 6.16: The results of the dynamic adaptation experiments.

Fig. 6.15). The value of μ is always 0.1, as in all our experiments. Each phase generates 2700 sessions, and differs from the previous one in one or two parameters (highlighted in the table). Each phase is divided into 9 epochs with 300 sessions each, for which the results are shown in Fig. 6.16.

Our experiments show that the infrastructure is always able to pick-up the best algorithm, so during the test run with the dynamic adaptation in place, the infrastructure achieves a higher percentage of successful sessions (75.6%) compared to the Locking (67.1%) and the Optimistic Validation (70.2%) tests, where the algorithms are fixed.

6.6 Chapter summary

In this chapter we have presented analytical models that characterize concurrent execution of web sessions with bounded inconsistency in shared data. The models predict the performance of the three concurrency control algorithms for web sessions — Optimistic Validation, No-Waiting Locking, and Pessimistic Admission Control — by computing the chosen metrics of interest, based on the information exposed by the *request flow* (Section 3.1) and *data access patterns* (Section 3.4) service access attributes. Namely, the models use as input the information about the CBMG request structure of user sessions and various timing parameters, which is gathered in real time by the Request Profiling Service. The information about the business-critical shared application data that the service provider needs to cover by data consistency constraints is specified by the service provider using the proposed flexible OP−COP−VALP model.

We augmented our JBoss middleware infrastructure with the web session concurrency control mechanisms, which enforce session data consistency constraints working only at the level of the abstract OP−COP−VALP model, with mappings of service requests to model operations specified by the service provider. This approach avoids the need to put concurrency control functionality in the application code and, more importantly, permits dynamic adaptation of concurrency control policies to changes in parameters of service usage, in order to maximize the metric of interest.

We have illustrated our models using the sample buyer scenario from the TPC-W e-Commerce benchmark, and have validated them by showing their close correspondence to measured results of concurrent session execution in both a simulated and a real web application server environment. We have also shown that our automated decision making middleware service is able to successfully choose, for the specified performance metric, the best concurrency control algorithm in real time in response to changing service usage patterns.

172

Chapter 7

Application Distribution

This chapter is focused on the problem of using component-based applications as the basis for distributed wide-area (edge) service deployment, a topic introduced earlier in Section 1.2.4. In Section 7.1 we formulate the service distribution problem in more detail. Section 7.2 presents our approach and methodology for addressing this problem. In Section 7.3 we describe the identified set of design rules and optimizations that enable beneficial and efficient distribution of component-based applications in wide area environments. These design rules rely upon the knowledge of *fine-grained resource utilization* and *data access patterns* of different service request types and reflect manual application of this knowledge during the process of application development in order to enable service distribution in wide-area networks. We present these design rules in an incremental fashion and show performance improvements achieved after each step.

7.1 Problem formulation

Application distribution and replication has become a noticeable trend in the way modern Internet services are designed and utilized. These techniques bring application data and data processing *closer to the clients* and help to cope, on the network level, with the unpredictable nature of Internet traffic, especially in wide-area environments, and, on the application level, with high-volume, widely varying, disparate client workloads. Examples of this approach vary from old-fashioned web caching of static content, to web content delivery using content-distribution networks (CDN), to distributed (edge) service deployment (Section 2.8).

Internet services built as component-based applications are natural candidates for service distribution, because component frameworks offer mechanisms enabling distributed application deployments. Despite their nominal suitability, component-based applications are traditionally deployed only in a centralized fashion in high-performance local area networks. In the rare cases when these applications are distributed in wide-area environments, the systems tend to be highly customized and handcrafted.

The advantages of distributing and replicating components across wide area environments are several. Cacheable components can be positioned in edge nodes, effectively bringing the service closer to clients, and thus improving not only client perceived latency, but also overall service availability since client requests can utilize several entry points into the service. Furthermore, specific "hot" components can be replicated and/or redeployed on-demand in new physical nodes in response to higher client loads or congested network links. Although component frameworks offer mechanisms to enable the distributed deployment of components, the primary challenge that needs to be addressed before wide-area deployments of general applications become commonplace is: how should component-based applications be engineered to enable efficient service distribution in heterogonous and high-latency network settings?

7.2   Approach and methodology

When a general component application is distributed in wide area environments, inter-component communication, otherwise "invisible" in local area networks, results in dramatically increased request response times, whose impact on overall application performance depends on what components and back-end datasources are accessed during a request's execution. Information of this kind belongs to the *fine-grained resource utilization* service access attribute (Section 3.3) and needs to be available for the service provider to be able to assess the performance quality of a distributed appli-

174

cation.

On the other hand, in order to ensure that popular or business critical service requests experience small response delays, the application should be *engineered* in a way that limits unnecessary wide area inter-component communication. To achieve this, the application developer needs to be aware of (1) the "read-write" data access behavior of service requests; and (2) whether or not the application state accessed in a request is shared among several clients. In other words, while developing the application, the developer needs to take into account the application *data access patterns*.

Our approach to enabling beneficial and efficient distribution of component-based applications in wide-area environments is to (1) take into account the information about read-write shared data access patterns and fine-grained resource utilization by service requests of different types and (2) based on this information, provide guidelines for application (re)structuring, which limits wide-area inter-component communication. To this end, we identify and recommend for use a small set of *design rules and optimizations for application structuring* that enable distribution of component-based applications: (1) Remote Façade design pattern, (2) Stateful Component Caching; (3) Query Caching, and (4) Asynchronous Updates.

We validate the applicability of these design rules by applying them to two sample Java EE component-based applications: Java Pet Store (Section 2.4.2) and RUBiS (Section 2.4.3). We deploy Java Pet Store and RUBiS in a fixed, simulated wide-area environment, apply the design patterns and optimizations in an incremental fashion, and after each step measure the performance of the application and draw conclusions about the impact of the changes.

7.2.1 Network topology

Our network topology aims at capturing a simple scaled-down wide-area distributed deployment of the test applications. The system consists of three JBoss application servers (see Section 2.3; we used JBoss version 2.4.4 with Jetty 3.1.3 web server, for the Java Pet Store tests and JBoss version 3.0.3 with Jetty 4.1.0, for the RUBiS tests) and a single database server

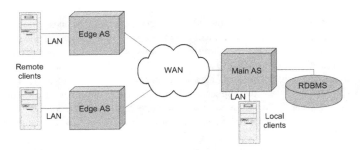

Figure 7.1: Network configuration for service distribution tests.

(MySQL version 4.0.12), each running on a dedicated 1GHz dual-processor Pentium III workstation. An emulated wide-area network (WAN) separates the three application servers. One of the application servers is located in the same LAN as the database server, hence acting as the **main server** of the system. Two other application servers act as **edge servers**. In addition, 9 client machines were used to generate client load, three for each application server. Clients machines are collocated with the corresponding server (sitting on the same LAN), emulating client load coming from users "close" to that server. The network topology was emulated by connecting all of the above nodes using a software router built using the *Click* modular router infrastructure [74]; traffic shaping components were used to simulate 100 ms latency each way in the WAN links, with 100 Mbit/s maximum combined network bandwidth (Fig. 7.1). In this work we don't address security issues, so we assume that edge servers are trusted entities.

7.2.2 Client simulation

While the overall performance of a component-based Internet service depends on its component distribution and combined client load, response times observed by clients also significantly depend on *client behavior*, as different types of users tend to access different web pages and, as a conse-

176

quence, different sets of service components are involved in a request's execution (Section 2.2.2). We divide all clients between two different *service usage (access) patterns* (Section 2.5.1): *Browser* and *Buyer* for Java Pet Store, and *Browser* and *Bidder* for RUBiS. Intuitively, the *Browser* pattern corresponds to *read-only* activities, while the *Buyer/Bidder* patterns are involved in *read-write* sessions. Considering different service usage patterns, first, helps to identify, which groups of clients benefit most from certain service distribution and replication, and second, provides an application deployer with the knowledge of *how* applications should be distributed and/or replicated, in order to be *adapted* to the needs of certain client groups.

Java Pet Store Browser. This pattern represents a user that merely *browses* the application web site in search of items of interest. This user neither logs in, nor buys any products. During our tests, we used Java Pet Store browser sessions consisting of 20 requests divided among the request types described in Table 7.1. Each session is a logically organized sequence of requests starting with the Main request. For example, an Item request always follows a Product request, with the requested item belonging to the previously requested product and category (see Section 2.4.2 for the description of application request types).

Java Pet Store Buyer. This pattern represents the behavior of a client who already knows what item(s) to buy. A buyer logs in, finds item(s) of interest, probably accessing a few product-related pages, puts desired items into the shopping cart, and checks them out. For the purpose of our tests, we organized Java Pet Store buyer sessions as a sequence of requests emphasizing a buyer's essential activities: Main, Signin, Verify Signin, Shopping Cart, Checkout, Place Order, Billing and Shipping, Commit Order, and Signout.

RUBiS Browser. This pattern represents, as in Java Pet Store, a user that merely *browses* the RUBiS web site and never bids on items. Our tests use RUBiS browser sessions of length 40, made up of individual requests with the weights shown in Table 7.2. Each session is a logically organized

Table 7.1: Breakdown of session requests by type, for Java Pet Store Browser.

Request type	Session request breakdown
Main	5%
Category	15%
Product	30%
Item	45%
Search	5%

Table 7.2: Breakdown of session requests by type, for RUBiS Browser.

Request type	Session request breakdown
Main	2.5%
Browse	2.5%
All Categories	2.5%
All Regions	2.5%
Region	2.5%
Category	7.5%
Category and Region	7.5%
Item	42.5%
Bids	15%
User Info	15%

sequence of requests starting with the Main request (see Section 2.4.3 for the description of application request types).

RUBiS Bidder. Unlike in Java Pet Store, where there is only one type of *"write"* activity — buying an item, in RUBiS, a user can *bid* on an item and *put* a comment for another user. For our tests, we organized RUBiS bidder sessions as a sequence of requests emphasizing these activities. A bidder bids on an item and leaves a comment for the seller of the item, with typical sessions involving the following requests: Main, Put Bid Auth, Put Bid Form, Store Bid, Put Comment Auth, Put Comment Form, and Store Comment.

In our tests, clients were divided between *Browsers* and *Buyers/Bidders* in the proportion of 80%/20%. We set the parameters of new session arrivals and inter-request times so that the combined client load remained steady at 30 requests per second, equally divided among all client groups. Each test lasted for approximately one hour, preceded by several minutes

Table 7.3: Average response times (in ms) for Java Pet Store Browser.

Configuration	Client	Request				
		Main	Category	Product	Item	Search
Centralized Pet Store	Local	87	95	94	88	106
(section 7.3.1)	Remote	488	492	492	486	496
Remote façade	Local	64	78	80	72	82
(section 7.3.2)	Remote	**72**	387	389	373	384
Stateful component	Local	55	82	84	55	77
caching (section 7.3.3)	Remote	55	394	390	**57**	393
Query caching	Local	56	50	51	54	87
(section 7.3.4)	Remote	55	**51**	**51**	55	481
Asynchronous updates	Local	61	54	53	57	92
(section 7.3.5)	Remote	59	51	53	58	459

of system "warm-up," if needed.

7.3 Design rules and optimizations

Tables 7.3, 7.4, 7.5, and 7.6 show average response times per request for the five Java Pet Store and RUBiS configurations described below, for the four types of clients described above — Java Pet Store Browser and Buyer and RUBiS Browser and Bidder (for request descriptions refer to Tables 2.2 and 2.4). Both **remote** group of clients (connecting to the **edge servers**) observed, as one would expect, practically equal response times, within a small error margin. Bold numbers indicate significant changes in performance, as compared to configurations appearing earlier in the table.

7.3.1 Centralized application

In the first experiment, we ran the centralized undistributed versions of Java Pet Store and RUBiS. In this configuration, the main server served all requests, whereas the edge servers were not used at all. This configuration represents the low end of the distribution spectrum, where effectively no

Table 7.4: Average response times (in ms) for Java Pet Store Buyer.

Configuration	Client	Main	S/in	Verif	Cart	Ch/out	Pl.Or.	Bill	Commit	S/out
						Request				
Centralized Pet Store (section 7.3.1)	Loc.	98	78	89	120	76	70	70	158	90
	Rem.	489	480	482	658	477	646	482	708	447
Remote façade (section 7.3.2)	Loc.	61	52	63	85	54	51	54	134	54
	Rem.	**60**	**54**	630	407	**61**	**57**	**61**	500	**63**
Stateful comp. caching (section 7.3.3)	Loc.	60	51	65	77	53	50	55	**584**	54
	Rem.	68	52	629	**80**	50	49	53	**950**	62
Query caching (section 7.3.4)	Loc.	58	51	61	70	50	50	54	614	52
	Rem.	61	49	638	69	51	52	53	966	54
Asynchronous updates (section 7.3.5)	Loc.	61	53	64	75	53	53	56	**195**	56
	Rem.	59	48	632	69	50	50	50	**536**	52

distribution takes place. As seen in the first two rows of Tables 7.3 – 7.6, accessing the service from a WAN link incurs approximately an extra 400 ms, which is due to two round trips: one for TCP handshaking and another for the HTTP request (we did not use keep-alive HTTP connections in our tests).

7.3.2 Remote façade

The centralized configuration suffers from two major problems. First, the system does not utilize all of its resources, since the edge servers are not being used at all. Second, HTTP requests going to the main server from remote clients incur significantly higher response times in comparison to local client requests. Both of these problems can be addressed by migrating part of the application components into the edge server.

The second configuration in our experiments was obtained by deploying

Table 7.5: Average response times (in ms) for RUBiS Browser.

Configu-ration	Client	Main	Browse	All Categ	All Regions	Region	Category	Categ & Reg	Item	Bids	User Info
Central.	Loc.	14	12	33	26	35	43	21	27	40	43
RUBiS	Rem.	421	414	434	438	434	649	426	430	446	452
Remote	Loc.	10	11	27	30	34	35	19	24	35	34
façade	Rem.	4	3	424	407	399	499	265	275	300	379
Stateful comp. caching	Loc.	13	16	29	32	39	38	23	19	30	31
	Rem.	3	3	423	463	435	526	279	7	323	404
Query	Loc.	9	12	12	15	17	16	12	15	16	16
caching	Rem.	5	4	7	7	7	6	5	8	8	8
Async.	Loc.	12	12	9	9	11	13	13	14	15	15
updates	Rem.	4	5	9	7	6	6	4	7	10	10

all web components (JSPs and servlets) and stateful session components in all three servers. This configuration addresses the problems of the previous centralized configuration by making better use of available resources and also bringing some of the application components closer to remote clients. However, wide-area HTTP requests are now substituted by possibly multiple wide-area inter-component RMI calls.

In addition to contributing to less maintainable, less reusable, and tightly coupled code, repeated fine-grained invocations of core components, such as entity EJBs, from front-end components (web tier) add the overhead of multiple network calls, and reduce concurrency at the server-side, since transactions effectively take longer to complete. A superior alternative is to wrap the domain model, typically implemented as a collection of possibly related entity beans, with a new thin layer of *façade objects* [53, 85]. Clients, who have access only to the façade, can delegate the execution of use cases in just one network call to the remote façade, which in turn

Table 7.6: Average response times (in ms) for RUBiS Bidder.

Configuration	Client		Request					
		Main	Put Bid Auth	Put Bid Form	Store Bid	Put Comm. Auth	Put Comm. Form	Store Comm.
Centralized	**Local**	12	13	32	36	13	25	35
RUBiS	**Remote**	419	419	439	437	414	432	432
Remote	**Local**	10	13	30	30	14	26	30
façade	**Remote**	**4**	**3**	408	284	**3**	284	282
Stateful comp.	**Local**	10	15	23	**372**	14	22	**377**
caching	**Remote**	4	4	450	**680**	4	303	**628**
Query	**Local**	9	10	15	377	9	16	374
caching	**Remote**	3	3	**7**	798	3	**6**	729
Async.	**Local**	10	15	15	**32**	9	10	**34**
updates	**Remote**	5	4	9	**421**	4	12	**419**

can perform multiple local calls needed to execute the use case against co-located domain objects. Besides reducing the number of remote method invocations, the façade provides a single entry point into the domain model, enabling improved transactional and security control. The pattern does not suggest a singleton façade responsible for the entire application; instead, multiple façade objects should be created to serve collections of related use cases. We discuss in more detail below, the modifications that were made to the test applications.

Java Pet Store. Pet Store uses stateful session beans (`ShoppingCart` and `ShoppingClientController`), which get deployed together with the stateless web components in all three servers. In the original Pet Store application, Category, Product, Item and Search requests present product information to end users, retrieving information from the Product database directly via JDBC. The lifecycle of opening, managing, and properly recycling database connections, as well as traversing query results demands verbose communication with the database server, resulting in overwhelm-

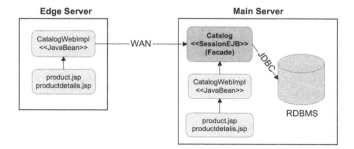

Figure 7.2: Implementation of the Remote Façade design pattern.

ingly degraded performance when the web tier and database are separated
by a high-latency network. As stated earlier, such scenarios can be easily
avoided by directing client requests to a façade that is co-located with the
database server. In our case, we substituted all direct database accesses
from the web layer with calls to the Catalog bean that served as a façade.
Furthermore, for all the request types used in our experiments, we rewrote
the application code so that every request included in the experiment incurs no more than one RMI call to shared components. The only exception
is the Verify Signin request, which makes two RMI calls, one to create a
Customer session bean for the customer that logged in, and another for
retrieving the customer's profile for future use.

To further reduce the number of remote method invocations, we used the
façade pattern in conjunction with caching of home and remote RMI stubs.
Home stubs were always cached to avoid unnecessary trips to the local
JNDI tree (*EJBHomeFactory* design pattern [85]). In the case of stateless
remote façades, remote stubs were pooled as well on the client side to avoid
the penalty incurred by the RMI call that initially creates the remote stub.
Fig. 7.2 illustrates an example of the use of the façade pattern for Java Pet
Store (for brevity, in the rest of the chapter, we will show such examples
only for the Java Pet Store application).

RUBiS. RUBiS does not use stateful session beans, so only web components were deployed in the edge servers. RUBiS required fewer code modifications because it already employed the *Session Façade* design pattern. Execution of use cases is delegated by web components to the façade session beans, collocated with the entity beans. Most of the changes resulted from the implementation of the *EJBHomeFactory* design pattern. Servlets now cached remote stubs of stateless session beans, while the latter cached home stubs of related entity beans, to reduce unnecessary lookups in the JNDI tree of the main server.

The average client response times for this configuration for the two applications are shown in Tables 7.3 – 7.6 (rows 3 and 4). Several points stand out from the measurements of this configuration:

- Many requests can be served completely using only session information stored in the edge server. This is particularly prominent in the case of the Pet Store buyer, where six out of nine requests can be served locally.

- If serving a request from a remote client requires going to the main server, a wide-area HTTP request in this configuration is substituted by one inter-component RMI call. In this case the façade design pattern does not itself significantly improve request response time, but it makes it minimal, keeping the number of wide-area RMI calls as small as possible.

- RMI can require more than one round trip for a single method invocation. It has been pointed out elsewhere that these shortcomings are mainly due to ping packets and distributed garbage collection [24]. Therefore, generally speaking, the benefits of the façade pattern are slightly diminished since RMI can incur more than one round trip per method invocation.

- The response times of local clients went down due to better load distribution.

184

7.3.3   Stateful Component Caching

In the previous configuration, all session-oriented stateful components were deployed in both servers, improving locality and load distribution. However, requests that trigger invocations on stateful components that are shared across multiple sessions did not gain much benefit from this approach. In the third configuration, we turn our attention to these shared stateful components, exemplified in Java EE by entity EJBs and relational database sources.

Our experience suggests that entity beans are excellent at handling heavy, concurrent transactional accesses, but they can be quite inefficient when used as data caches. As a matter of fact, this is clearly manifested in the lifecycle and transactional management specifications of entity beans, and it simply reflects design choices made by the EJB architects. However, data locality is critical when it comes to efficient wide-area service partitioning. Fortunately, entity beans can be easily transformed into data caches by minor modifications to their lifecycle definition. As a matter of fact, most application server vendors already support some form of read-only entity beans with a timeout invalidation mechanism, and in some cases they also support a programmatic invalidation interface.

Common to all the current approaches for updating read-only beans is that, upon invalidation, the read-only bean refreshes itself with the database using a pull protocol. This approach works well in a local-area setting, where the read-only bean communication overhead with the database is negligible, but as stated earlier, it results in unacceptable performance in the wide-area. To avoid opening and maintaining remote database connections, read-only beans can efficiently refresh their content by querying a remote façade upon the first business method call after the invalidation. Another approach would be to *push the updated state* to read-only beans, with the updated state specified as a parameter of the invalidation call. This push-based scheme has the major advantage that clients of read-only beans would always see local response times, which is not the case with the pull-based approach. At first sight, it might seem that since the push-based scheme is not demand-driven, it can result in sending superfluous updates. However, the number of RMI calls is the same in both cases, because the invalidation

185

call has to be made anyway. The push-based scheme ends up transferring more data, but this is a small price to pay for significantly improving the response time of remote clients. Furthermore, several simple and effective optimizations can be applied, such as: transferring only the changes instead of the entire bean's state (i.e., fields that were modified), and compressing large fields for better bandwidth utilization. Moreover, in most cases the bandwidth problem is not as relevant, since more than half of the data traffic incurred by RMI ends up being due to distributed garbage collection [24].

The above insights can be materialized in a version of the so-called *Read-Mostly Pattern* [75] where transactional operations are sent to the read-write version of the bean, which is typically co-located with the data-source; non-transactional read operations are handled locally by the read-only cache. In addition, upon write operations, the read-write components push the updates across the wide-area to the edge read-only beans. In this configuration we strive for zero staleness: read-write entity beans block while the update is pushed to the read-only beans, hence a read operation that arrives after a previous write has committed, will always read the correct value.

Java Pet Store. The following changes were made to Java Pet Store in addition to the last façade configuration, to implement stateful component caching:

- Three new read-write entity beans were introduced: `Category`, `Product`, and `Item`. These beans implement functionality that was previously handled by the `Catalog` bean, which accessed the product database directly via JDBC.

- Read-only versions of `Category`, `Product`, `Item`, and `Inventory` beans were introduced.

- A blocking push-based update mechanism was implemented between read-write beans and their read-only counterparts. The updates make use of a remote façade so that each update incurs only one RMI call.

- The `Catalog` bean delegates to the newly introduced entity beans.

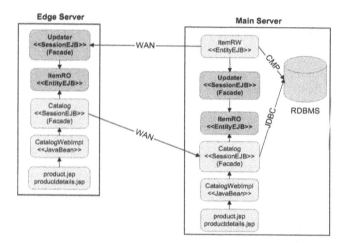

Figure 7.3: Implementation of Stateful Component Caching.

- The read-only beans and the `Catalog` bean were also deployed on the edge servers. The edge `Catalog` bean also has a reference to the central `Catalog` bean. If a request that comes to the edge `Catalog` bean cannot be served locally by delegating to the read-only beans, it would be dispatched to the central `Catalog` bean, which is co-located with the database. For example, aggregate queries are always delegated to the central `Catalog` bean since they need to be executed in the database server.

Analogous code modifications, introducing read-only versions of Entity EJBs and a blocking push-based update mechanism, were introduced into RUBiS. Figure 7.3 illustrates the read-mostly pattern for the `Item` EJB of the Java Pet Store application. Average response times for this configuration are shown in Tables 7.3 – 7.6 (rows 5 and 6). Several conclusions can be drawn from the measurements of this configuration:

- Zero staleness for browsers comes at a performance price for buyers/bidders, since they have to block while the updates are being pushed across the wide-area to the edge servers. More specifically, in Java Pet Store, the Commit request of the buyer session updates the `Inventory` bean and hence the response time for this request is significantly higher than in the previous configuration for both local and remote buyers. The same effect is seen for the Store Bid and Store Comment requests of the RUBiS bidder session.

- Even though the Pet Store buyer response time for the Commit request is higher, the overall average is not affected so much since the buyer's Shopping Cart request can be served locally by the newly introduced read-only beans. In contrast, the RUBiS bidder average response time increased, because the bidder does not benefit from read-only beans, but needs to block on the Store Bid and Store Comment requests.

- The Item request of both Pet Store and RUBiS browser sessions makes full use of read-only entity beans and so has local response time, but the other requests still need to go to the main server to execute aggregate SQL queries.

- The response time for the Pet Store and RUBiS Item request is slightly improved for the local browser due to read-only bean caching, which replaces database access in the original configuration.

7.3.4 Query Caching

Entity bean instances typically correspond to rows in a database table, implying that aggregate queries can only be executed by a relational database system. The root of the problem is the well-known incompatibility (impedance mismatch) between object-oriented languages and SQL. In Java Pet Store and RUBiS, as in most web-based e-Commerce applications, aggregate queries constitute a large part of application data retrievals, and hence *caching of query results* in edge servers can further reduce the number of remote method invocations to components that are co-located with centralized database servers. The benefits of caching query results in a local scale

188

are less important because modern database servers are typically equipped with sophisticated query caching mechanisms, and possess all the information needed to make optimal caching decisions.

A general problem with caching query results is determining which queries are affected by changes that occur to the database. This is a well-researched problem [38] and we do not make any contribution to this field, nor try to incorporate any advanced query caching techniques in our experiments. Our focus is on the benefits of caching aggregate SQL query results at edge servers to avoid expensive trips to remote data centers. A straightforward implementation would be to use a demand-driven, pull-based update mechanism, whereby upon receiving the first read request after invalidation, the query cache manager gets the latest updates by re-executing the query in the remote database. Alternatively, a push-based protocol can be used that eagerly sends updates to the query cache manager. This scheme has the following benefits over the pull-based approach: (1) query readers are not penalized, because they never trigger requests to the remote database; (2) updates are typically small (usually involving single rows), hence making it easier to propagate only partial information [38] instead of re-sending the entire query result, effectively reducing bandwidth consumption.

Java Pet Store.   We cache the results of two queries in the Java Pet Store application: the set of products for a given category, and the set of items belonging to a given product. These queries are heavily used by the Category and Product requests of the browser session, and hence caching them in the edge server avoids remote method invocations to the main server. The query result cache was incorporated in the `Catalog` bean. For simplicity, we implemented the pull-based update mechanism for caching query results. However, the impact of invalidations is not visible in our test results, because the catalog of Java Pet Store is read-only.

RUBiS.   We implemented caching of all queries involved in the processing of all requests in our browser and bidders sessions. The query result caches were naturally incorporated in those stateless session beans that make cor-

189

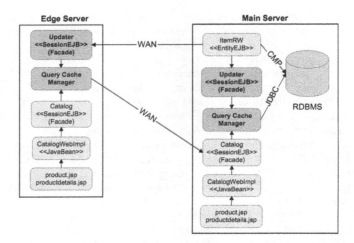

Figure 7.4: Implementation of Query Caching.

responding finder method invocations (queries) on entity bean home interfaces. A push-based query update mechanism was implemented, and it makes use of the *remote façade* design pattern, namely updates to read-only beans and query caches are made in one bulk RMI call from the main server.

Figure 7.4 shows relevant components deployed on the main and edge servers, for the Java Pet Store application. Average response times for this configuration are shown in Tables 7.3 – 7.6 (rows 7 and 8). The following observations can be made from the measurements of this configuration:

- As expected, query result caching lowers both Java Pet Store and RUBiS remote browser response times. This is especially seen in the performance of RUBiS remote browser, now indistinguishable from the local browser. Also query caching has a positive local effect, since it reduces required database accesses.

- The Java Pet Store Search request performs a keyword query, which

190

is not cached, and hence it still incurs the cost of the remote call to the database façade.

- Pet Store buyer's and RUBiS bidder's performance does not improve because they still block on updates.

7.3.5 Asynchronous Updates

Achieving zero staleness for browsers penalizes the buyer/bidder, who blocks while the update is propagated across the wide-area to the edge read-only beans. This approach also suffers from severe scalability issues, since the response time for write operations is proportional to the number of individual fine-grained updates triggered by a single façade call. As a matter of fact, this is the case with the Pet Store buyer's Commit Order request, which causes writes to the Inventory EJB for each item in the user's shopping cart. This negative effect is not noticeable in our test results, because we never put more than one item in the shopping cart.

Pushing updates in an *asynchronous* fashion eliminates this performance bottleneck. Upon transaction commit, updates are asynchronously pushed across the wide-area to the edge read-only components. But is the staleness of asynchronous updates acceptable? Read-only beans and aggregate SQL query results typically contain data, which is displayed to the user in a tabular format. Even if the web tier components obtained this data from the transactional read-write version of the bean or the database, the information will likely be stale due to the incurred communication overhead, user think time, and other concurrent server activity. In a sense, the staleness of shared presentation data is unavoidable, and the asynchronous updates design optimization takes advantage of this fact to significantly improve response times.

The only change from the last configuration was to substitute the synchronous update façade with an asynchronous message-driven bean (MDB) façade that propagates updates to both read-only beans and query caches. The read-write beans publish their updates in a local topic, where multiple edge cache updaters are subscribed. This approach completely avoids the blocking problem and its scalability is limited only by the messaging

191

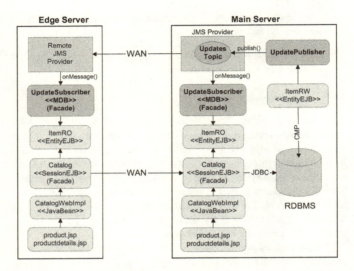

Figure 7.5: Implementation of the Asynchronous Updates design optimization.

middleware.

Figure 7.5 shows a partial snapshot of the Java Pet Store component graph. Average response times for this configuration are shown in Tables 7.3 – 7.6 (rows 9 and 10). Some remarks about the numbers follow:

- The most noticeable impact of asynchronous updates as compared to the previous configuration is improved Pet Store buyer and RUBiS bidder response times.

- The remote buyer/bidder still incurs wide-area latencies in some of the requests since it requires read-write access to shared components residing in the main server. However, these are unavoidable and typically represent only a very small fraction of the overall request mix.

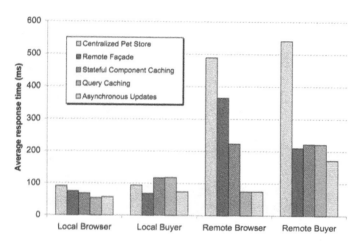

Figure 7.6: Java Pet Store session average response times.

7.3.6 Evaluation summary

Figures 7.6 and 7.7 summarize the results obtained from our tests. The last configuration achieves the best overall performance and scalability by accumulating all improvements. The *Remote Façade* design pattern avoids unnecessary remote method invocations and implicitly defines the optimal application partitioning granularity. The use of this pattern is required if communicating components are separated by a wide-area network, regardless of the nature of user requests served by these components. *Read-only entity beans* and *query caches* deployed in edge servers absorb the load generated by remote clients and save expensive trips to centralized data centers. *Asynchronous propagation of updates* achieves scalability and guarantees that updaters are not penalized by blocking on write operations.

The overall effect of applied design patterns and optimizations is twofold. First and foremost, remote clients are almost completely insulated from wide-area effects. In the few cases when remote clients incur wide-

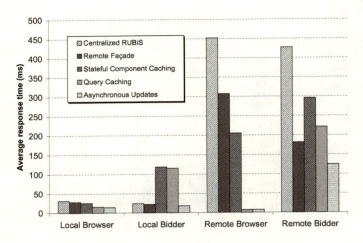

Figure 7.7: RUBiS session average response times.

area inter-component RMI calls, the communication overhead is as small as possible due to the façade pattern. Secondly, both local and remote clients experience improved performance due to aggressive caching of stateful components.

7.3.7 Pattern implementation automation

Whereas the correct implementation of the façade pattern largely remains the responsibility of application developers, container environments can and should automate transparent caching of stateful shared components. The system infrastructure for this purpose should consist of (1) *extended deployment descriptors* specification and (2) *general and flexible container environments* supporting this specification and implementing its functionality.

Let us revisit the example of read-only entity beans optimization (Section 7.3.3). The extended deployment descriptor of an entity bean should

194

specify whether the bean is deployed in *read-write* or *read-only* mode. In the latter case, the deployment descriptor should identify the updater read-write bean and the method of update (synchronous vs. asynchronous). Any application-specific relaxed consistency parameters (Section 2.7.3) should also go here. The container infrastructure in turn should transparently link the read-write entity bean containers with the corresponding read-only containers to enable propagation of updates.

The caching of query results can also be automated by container infrastructures. Currently, EJB containers do not support query caching, as that is typically left to database servers. Even though it is natural to let the database server transparently handle query caching, this approach does not improve data locality across wide-area environments. The problem is exacerbated due to the so-called $n+1$ *database calls problem* [85], which reflects the fact that with certain EJB implementations, executing a single aggregate query that returns n rows could require $n+1$ database calls (see also Section 5.3). Due to the unacceptable incurred overhead caused by this impedance mismatch issues, it is desirable to have separate containers for handling read-only aggregate queries. These containers should handle query result caching and invalidation transparently using application-specific information from extended deployment descriptors. This information should identify the queries to be cached and the invalidation mechanism. Moreover, operations (of possibly other components) that cause query result invalidations/updates should be specified as well.

As a result of pattern implementation automation, application developers would be freed from implementing tricky update mechanisms that require the deployment of additional auxiliary components such as message-driven beans and JMS topics, needed for example, for the implementation of the Asynchronous Updates optimization (Section 7.3.5). Another advantage of this approach is that it would allow dynamic adaptation of component-based applications achieved through demand-driven (re)deployment of additional application components as appropriate for changing environment conditions and service usage patterns. However, in order to achieve such dynamic adaptation, one needs robust mechanisms that would automate the process of application component deployment/undeployment.

Our work in [8, 93] addressed this aspect, by introducing an infrastructure for automatic dynamic deployment of Java EE applications in distributed environments.

7.4 Chapter summary

In this chapter we have discussed the problem of using component-based applications for distributed wide-area (edge) service deployments. We have identified and recommended for use a small set of generally-applicable design rules for orchestrating inter-component interactions and managing component state, which limits wide-area inter-component communication and therefore enables beneficial and efficient service distribution in wide area environments: (1) Remote Façade design pattern, (2) Stateful Component Caching; (3) Query Caching, and (4) Asynchronous Updates.

We have validated the applicability of the proposed design rules by applying them to several prototypical Java EE component-based applications in an incremental fashion and showing achieved performance improvements. Our test results present strong experimental evidence that component-based applications can be efficiently distributed in wide-area environments. More specifically, applications whose typical user sessions do not require heavy transactional access to centralized data and involve user think time can be engineered so that the cost of remote service accesses is absorbed by edge deployment of stateful session components and shared non-transactional caches.

In all cases, the identified design optimizations and their use in particular application scenarios are driven by the information about *data access patterns* (Section 3.4) and *fine-grained resource utilization* (Section 3.3) by service requests of different types.

196

Chapter 8

Conclusions and Directions for Future Research

This chapter summarizes the work presented in this book, draws important conclusions, and identifies interesting directions for future research.

8.1 Summary

There are several reasons why it is difficult to provision and manage modern component-based Internet services so that they provide stable quality-of-service (QoS) guarantees to their clients. First, component middleware are complex software systems that expose several *configurable application runtime policies* and *server resource management mechanisms*, which can be independently tuned to improve service performance and optimize server resource utilization. Second, *session-oriented client behavior* with *complex data access patterns* makes it hard to predict what impact tuning these policies and mechanisms has on application behavior. Finally, modern component-based applications themselves exhibit *complex structural organization* with requests of different types using different middleware services and accessing different application components and datasources; moreover, these components could be distributed and/or replicated for failover, performance, or business purposes.

In this book, we have looked at various solutions that alleviate this

197

situation by targeting three interconnected goals: (1) providing improved QoS guarantees to the clients of component-based services; (2) optimizing server resource utilization; and (3) providing application developers with guidelines for natural application structuring, which enable efficient use of the state-of-the-art mechanisms for improving service performance. Specifically, we explored the claim that **exposing and using detailed information about how clients use component-based Internet services enables mechanisms that achieve the range of goals listed above.** We validated this claim by showing its applicability to the following four problems:

1. Maximizing reward brought by Internet services.

2. Optimizing utilization of server resource pools.

3. Providing web session data integrity guarantees.

4. Enabling Internet service distribution in wide-area environments.

The techniques that we have described and evaluated are applicable at both the *application structuring* stage and the *application operation* stage, and range from automatic (i.e., performed by middleware in real time) to manual (i.e., involve the programmer, or the service provider). These techniques take into account service usage information exposed at different levels, ranging from high-level structure of user sessions to low level information about resource consumption by different request types. We have identified four related groups of *service access attributes*, that correspond to different levels of service usage information: (1) request flow, (2) coarse-grained resource utilization and "reward," (3) fine-grained server resource utilization, and (4) data access patterns. Some of this information can be automatically obtained by request profiling, some can be obtained by statically analyzing the application structure, while some needs to be specified by the service provider.

Together, these pieces of information help to (1) achieve optimal utilization of pooled server resources; (2) enable automated middleware decision making processes that choose an appropriate resource management mechanism in real time, in response to changing service usage patterns; and (3)

198

improve performance by up to two times for centralized applications and by up to 8 times for distributed ones.

8.2 Conclusions

In this book, we have presented a set of models, techniques, middleware mechanisms, and application design rules, showing that exposing and using detailed information about session-oriented usage of component-based Internet services by their clients helps to improve performance and manageability of these services. Specifically, the contributions of this work are the following:

Models and techniques.

- Reward-driven session prioritization schemes, which show their utility for improving the QoS delivered to users that bring the most profit to the Internet service, and for maximizing profit attained by the service in the overload situations.

- A model of request execution with 2-tier exclusive server resource holding (threads, database connections), which enables accurate prediction of the optimal configuration for the thread and database connection pools in component application servers, for a given mix of client requests.

- Analytical models of concurrent web session execution with bounded inconsistency in shared application data, which are able to accurately predict the values of QoS metrics of interest.

Middleware mechanisms.

- Middleware request profiling infrastructure, which permits one to obtain service usage information at different levels without imposing significant performance overheads.

- A set of middleware decision-making mechanisms (e.g., request prioritization, automatic concurrency control for web sessions, etc.), implemented in a modular, extensible, and pluggable fashion with minimal, backward compatible, changes to the original web application server code. These mechanisms show their effectiveness in making run-time resource-utilization decisions and in determining the optimal configuration of critical server resources, without significant performance and management overheads. We have implemented and evaluated the mechanisms in a production-level application server JBoss, which utilizes the Java EE component model.

Application design rules.

- A set of application design rules that enable beneficial and efficient distribution of component-based Internet services in wide area environments.

Different parties involved in different stages of a component-based Internet service lifecycle could benefit from different aspects of the work presented in this book. Application developers could benefit from using the described set of application design rules and optimizations for building component-based applications. Middleware architects and developers could benefit from utilizing the set of described middleware mechanisms to introduce their functionality into the middleware systems. Service operators (e.g., system administrators) could benefit from using the described models and techniques in order to boost performance of component-based Internet services and improve their manageability, given that these mechanisms and the corresponding functionality is provided by the underlying middleware.

For demonstration and evaluation purposes, in this book we have used the Java EE component framework, which is currently the most popular and widely used component framework in the enterprise arena. However, we believe that most of the described techniques and mechanisms are applicable to other component frameworks as well, such as the CORBA Component Model (CCM) and .NET. Moreover, certain techniques and mechanisms described in this book, such as for example, Reward-Driven Request

Prioritization, are general enough to be applicable to web servers and middleware utilizing other technologies.

8.3 Directions for future research

Given that the *internal* complexity of data-centric Internet services and their hosting environments will likely only grow in the future, the only way to render efficient management and beneficial utilization of these systems is to curtail their *external* complexity, as it is exposed to the system administrators. One way to limit the exposed management complexity of the service is to *automate* some of the service management aspects, which contrasts with current primarily manual approaches for the same task.

Such automation is impossible without additional information of some kind that could be used to "drive" or "guide" the service management process. As the work presented in this book has shown, a great deal of such information can be extracted from service usage information. There is a benefit in thinking of the use of this information along a continuous spectrum, ranging from fully automatic techniques to fully manual ones. We believe that the most useful techniques would lie somewhere in the middle of the spectrum, representing semi-automatic service management techniques.

Some interesting directions for future research in the area of middleware-based Internet services are described below.

- One promising direction for future research is to look at how one could automate the Internet service distribution process. In this book, we have shown that a set of reusable application design rules and optimizations, based on generic data access patterns, can be applied to enable efficient and beneficial service distribution. However, the implementation of these policies is left to the application programmer. We believe that some of the service distribution decisions can be automated (at least partly) through some combination of profile-based learning and template-based code generation, where the application programmer would need only to write the "skeletons" of application components, and the middleware would instantiate the actual component "realizations" based on the data access patterns, typical for the specific application and the execution environment.

- One of the characteristics of modern Internet services is the *gap* between the level at which *user objectives, expectations and goals are expressed or specified,* and the level at which *the mechanisms that achieve these goals operate.* For example, the level of QoS specification (e.g., request response times, request throughput) is not compatible with the level of server resource management (e.g., thread and database connection pool size, caching policies, etc.), that influences QoS. We believe that bridging this gap requires a combination of analytical modeling of the kind presented in this book, and the design of appropriate mechanisms and policies to automate application configuration and management decisions.

- Modern Internet services are typically expected to be running for long periods of time, during which the client behavior can change significantly. It is impossible to find the configuration of the service that would perform optimally during the whole duration of service uptime. There is a need to "continuously refine" the performance of the service. We believe that this is possible to do based on logging of various user actions. One can think of a service that starts off with a default configuration, but after some time recognizes which management policies are more beneficial for service performance and converges to these. Of interest here is the possibility that one can "actively probe" how certain service management policies are performing. Designing such probes and finding ways to use the inferred information in a way that avoids exhaustive search of the best policies, represent interesting and challenging problems.

References

[1] T. F. Abdelzaher and K. G. Shin. QoS provisioning with qContracts in web and multimedia servers. In *Proceedings of the IEEE Real-Time Systems Symposium (RTSS'99)*, December 1999.

[2] T. F. Abdelzaher, K. G. Shin, and N. Bhatti. Performance guarantees for web server end-systems: A control-theoretical approach. *IEEE Transactions on Parallel and Distributed Systems*, 13(1):80–96, 2002.

[3] D. Agrawal, A. El Addadi, and A. K. Singh. Consistency and orderability: Semantics-based correctness criteria for databases. *ACM Transactions On Database Systems*, 18(3):460–486, 1993.

[4] R. Agrawal, M. Carey, and M. Livny. Concurrency control performance modeling: Alternatives and implications. *ACM Transactions on Database Systems*, 12(4):609–654, 1987.

[5] L. V. Ahlfors. *Complex Analysis*. McGraw–Hill, 1979.

[6] Akamai Technologies Inc. http://www.akamai.com/.

[7] Akamai Technologies Inc. EdgeSuite Enterprise Edition. http://www.akamai.com/html/solutions/.

[8] A. Akkerman, A. Totok, and V. Karamcheti. Infrastructure for automatic dynamic deployment of J2EE applications in distributed environments. In *Proceedings of the 3rd International Working Conference on Component Deployment (CD'2005)*, November 2005.

[9] J. Almedia, M. Dabu, A. Manikntty, and P. Cao. Providing differentiated levels of service in web content hosting. In *Proceedings of the First Workshop on Internet Server Performance*, June 1998.

[10] V. Almeida, M. Crovella, A. Bestravos, and A. Oliveira. Characterizing reference locality in the WWW. In *Proceedings of the IEEE/ACM International Conference on Parallel and Distributed Information Systems (PDIS'96)*, December 1996.

[11] M. Arlitt. Characterizing web user sessions. In *Proceedings of the Performance and Architecture of Web Servers Workshop*, June 2000.

[12] M. Arlitt, D. Krishnamurthy, and J. Rolia. Characterizing the scalability of a large web-based shopping system. *ACM Transactions on Internet Technology*, 1(1):44–69, 2001.

[13] M. Arlitt and C. Williamson. Web server workload characterization. In *Proceedings of the ACM SIGMETRICS Conference on Measurement and Modeling of Computer Systems*, May 1996.

[14] B. R. Badrinath and K. Ramamritham. Semantics-based concurrency control: Beyond commutativity. *ACM Transactions on Database Systems*, 17(1):163–199, 1992.

[15] P. Barford, A. Bestravos, A. Bradley, and M. Crovella. Changes in web client access patterns: Characteristics and caching implications. *World Wide Web Journal*, 2(1):15–28, 1999.

[16] P. Barford and M. Crovella. Generating representative web workloads for network and server performance evaluation. In *Proceedings of the ACM SIGMETRICS Conference on Measurement and Modeling of Computer Systems*, June 1998.

[17] N. S. Barghouti and G. E. Kaiser. Concurrency control in advanced database applications. *ACM Computing Surveys*, 23(3):269–317, 1991.

[18] B. Bennett, B. Hahm, A. Leff, T. Mikalsen, K. Rasmus, J. Rayfield, and I. Rouvellou. A distributed object-oriented framework to offer

transactional support for long-running business processes. In *Proceedings of the 2nd ACM/IFIP/USENIX International Middleware Conference*, April 2000.

[19] P. Bernstein and E. Newcomer. *Principles Of Transaction Processing*. Morgan Kaufmann Publishers, 1997.

[20] N. Bhatti and R. Friedrich. Web server support for tiered services. *IEEE Network*, 13(5):64–71, 1999.

[21] P. Bhoj, S. Ramanathan, and S. Singhal. Web2K: Bringing QoS to web servers. HP Laboratories Technical Report HPL-2000-61, May 2000.

[22] P. Brebner and S. Ran. Entity bean A, B, C's: Enterprise JavaBeans commit options and caching. In *Proceedings of the 3rd ACM/IFIP/USENIX International Middleware Conference*, November 2001.

[23] L. Breslau, P. Cao, L. Fan, G. Phillips, and S. Shenker. Web caching and Zipf-like distributions: Evidence and implications. In *Proceedings of the IEEE Conference on Computer Communications (INFOCOM'99)*, March 1999.

[24] S. Campadello, O. Koskimies, K. Raatikainen, and H. Helin. Wireless Java RMI. In *Proceedings of the 4th International Enterprise Distributed Object Computing Conference (EDOC'00)*, September 2000.

[25] J. Carlstrom and R. Rom. Application-aware admission control and scheduling in web servers. In *Proceedings of the IEEE Conference on Computer Communications (INFOCOM'02)*, June 2002.

[26] E. Cecchet, J. Marguerite, and W. Zwaenepoel. Performance and scalability of EJB applications. In *Proceedings of the 17th ACM Conference on Object-Oriented Programming, Systems, Languages and Applications (OOPSLA'02)*, November 2002.

[27] J. Challenger, P. Dantzig, and A. Iyengar. A scalable and highly available system for serving dynamic data at frequently accessed web sites. In *Proceedings of the High Performance Networking and Computing Conference (SC'98)*, November 1998.

[28] A. Chankhunthod, P. Danzig, C. Neerdaels, M. Schwartz, and K. Worrell. A hierarchical Internet object cache. In *Proceedings of the USENIX Annual Technical Conference*, January 1996.

[29] H. Chen and A. Iyengar. A tiered system for serving differentiated content. *World Wide Web Journal*, 6(4):331–352, 2003.

[30] H. Chen and P. Mohapatra. Session-based overload control in QoS-aware web servers. In *Proceedings of the IEEE Conference on Computer Communications (INFOCOM'02)*, June 2002.

[31] M. Chen, E. Kiciman, E. Fratkin, E. Brewer, and A. Fox. Pinpoint: Problem determination in large, dynamic, Internet services. In *Proceedings of the International Conference on Dependable Systems and Networks (DSN'02)*, June 2002.

[32] X. Chen, H. Chen, and P. Mohapatra. An admission control scheme for predictable server response time for web accesses. In *Proceedings of the International World Wide Web Conference (WWW'01)*, May 2001.

[33] L. Cherkasova. Scheduling strategy to improve response time for web applications. In *Proceedings of the International Conference on High Performance Computing and Networking (HPCN Europe'98)*, April 1998.

[34] L. Cherkasova and P. Phaal. Session-based admission control: A mechanism for peak load management of commercial web sites. *IEEE Transactions on Computers*, 51(6):669–685, 2002.

[35] M. Crovella and A. Bestavros. Self-similarity in World Wide Web traffic: Evidence and possible causes. In *Proceedings of the ACM*

SIGMETRICS Conference on Measurement and Modeling of Computer Systems, May 1996.

[36] M. Crovella, R. Frangioso, and M. Harchol-Balter. Connection scheduling in web servers. In *Proceedings of the USENIX Symposium on Internet Technologies and Systems (USITS99)*, October 1999.

[37] U. Dayal, M. Hsu, and R. Ladin. A transactional model for long-running activities. In *Proceedings of the 17th International Conference on Very Large Databases (VLDB'91)*, September 1991.

[38] L. Degenaro, A. Iyengar, I. Lipkind, and I. Rouvellou. A middleware system which intelligently caches query results. In *Proceedings of the 2nd ACM/IFIP/USENIX International Middleware Conference*, April 2000.

[39] L. C. DiPippo and V. F. Wolfe. Object-based semantic real-time concurrency control with bounded imprecision. *Knowledge and Data Engineering*, 9(1):135–147, 1997.

[40] F. Douglis, A. Feldmann, B. Krishnamurthy, and J. Mogul. Rate of change and other metrics: A live study of the World Wide Web. In *Proceedings of the USENIX Symposium on Internet Technologies and Systems (USITS'97)*, December 1997.

[41] R. Doyle, J. Chase, O. Asad, W. Jin, and A. Vahdat. Model-based resource provisioning in a web service utility. In *Proceedings of the USENIX Symposium on Internet Technologies and Systems (USITS'03)*, March 2003.

[42] eBay Inc. http://www.ebay.com.

[43] Edge Side Includes (ESI). http://www.esi.org/.

[44] L. Eggert and J. Heidemann. Application-level differentiated services for web servers. *World Wide Web Journal*, 3(2):133–142, 1999.

[45] S. Elnikety, E. Nahum, J. Tracey, and W. Zwaenepoel. A method for transparent admission control and request scheduling in dynamic e-Commerce web sites. In *Proceedings of the International World Wide Web Conference (WWW'04)*, May 2004.

[46] L. Fan, P. Cao, J. Almeida, and A. Z. Broder. Summary cache: a scalable wide-area web-cache sharing protocol. Technical Report 1361, CS Department, University of Wisconsin, Madison, February 1998.

[47] A. A. Farrag and M. T. Ozsu. Using semantic knowledge of transactions to increase concurrency. *ACM Transactions On Database Systems*, 14(4):503–525, 1989.

[48] M. Fleury. JBoss Blue Paper. http://www.jboss.org.

[49] M. Fleury and F. Reverbel. The JBoss extensible server. In *Proceedings of the 4th ACM/IFIP/USENIX International Middleware Conference*, June 2003.

[50] I. Foster, C. Kesselman, and S. Tuecke. The anatomy of the Grid: Enabling scalable virtual organizations. *The International Journal of High Performance Computing Applications*, 15(3):200–222, 2001.

[51] M. J. Freedman, E. Freudenthal, and D. Mazieres. Democratizing content publication with Coral. In *Proceedings of the USENIX Symposium on Networked Systems Design and Implementation (NSDI'04)*, March 2004.

[52] X. Fu, W. Shi, A. Akkerman, and V. Karamcheti. CANS: Composable adaptive network services infrastructure. In *Proceedings of the USENIX Symposium on Internet Technologies and Systems (USITS'01)*, March 2001.

[53] E. Gamma, R. Helm, R. Johnson, and J. Vlissides. *Design Patterns: Elements of Reusable Object-Oriented Software*. Addison-Wesley, New York, 1994.

[54] L. Gao, M. Dahlin, A. Nayate, J. Zheng, and A. Iyengar. Application specific data replication for edge services. In *Proceedings of the International World Wide Web Conference (WWW'03)*, May 2003.

[55] H. Garcia-Molina. Using semantic knowledge for transaction processing in a distributed database. *ACM Transactions On Database Systems*, 8(2):186–213, 1983.

[56] H. Garcia-Molina, D. Gawlick, J. Klein, K. Kleissner, and K. Salem. Modeling long-running activities as nested sagas. *Data Engineering*, 14(1):14–18, 1991.

[57] H. Garcia-Molina and K. Salem. Sagas. In *Proceedings of the ACM International Conference on Management of Data (SIGMOD'87)*, May 1987.

[58] J. Gray and A. Reuter. *Transaction Processing: Concepts And Techniques*. Morgan Kaufmann Publishers, 1993.

[59] S. Gribble, M. Welsh, R. von Behren, E. Brewer, D. Culler, N. Borisov, S. Czerwinski, R. Gummadi, J. Hill, A. Joseph, R. Katz, Z. M. Mao, S. Ross, and B. Zhao. The Ninja architecture for robust Internet-scale systems and services. *Computer Networks*, 35(4):473–497, 2001.

[60] D. Gross and C.M. Harris. *Fundamentals of Queueing Theory*. John Wiley & Sons, 1974.

[61] GVU's WWW User Surveys. http://www.gvu.gatech.edu/user_surveys/.

[62] J. R. Haritsa, M. J. Carey, and M. Livny. On being optimistic about real-time constraints. In *Proceedings of the 9th Symposium on Principles of Database Systems (PODS'90)*, April 1990.

[63] M. Herlihy. Extending multiversion time-stamping protocols to exploit type information. *IEEE Transactions on Computers*, 36(4):443–448, 1987.

[64] M. Herlihy. Apologizing versus asking permission: Optimistic concurrency control for abstract data types. *ACM Transactions on Database Systems*, 15(1):96–124, 1990.

[65] IBM corporation. WebSphere Platform. `http://www.ibm.com/websphere`.

[66] A.-A. Ivan, J. Harman, M. Allen, and V. Karamcheti. Partitionable Services: A framework for seamlessly adapting distributed applications to heteregeneous environments. In *Proceedings of the 11th IEEE International Symposium on High Performance Distributed Computing (HPDC'02)*, July 2002.

[67] S. Jajodia and L. Kerschberg. *Advanced Transaction Models And Architectures*. Kluwer Academic Publishers, 1997.

[68] JBoss Java Application Server. `http://www.jboss.org`.

[69] Jetty HTTP Server and Servlet Container. `http://jetty.mortbay.org`.

[70] G. E. Kaiser. Cooperative transactions for multiuser environments. In *Won Kim (Ed.), Modern Database Systems: The Object Model, Interoperability, and Beyond*, pages 409–433. ACM Press and Addison-Wesley, 1995.

[71] A. Kamra, V. Misra, and E. Nahum. Yaksha: A self-tuning controller for managing the performance of 3-tiered web sites. In *Proceedings of the 12th IEEE International Workshop on Quality of Service (IWQoS'04)*, June 2004.

[72] D. R. Kincaid and E. W. Cheney. *Numerical Analysis: Mathematics of Scientific Computing*. Brooks Cole, 2001.

[73] L. Kleinrock. *Queueing Systems*. John Wiley & Sons, 1975.

[74] E. Kohler, R. Morris, B. Chen, J. Jannotti, and M. F. Kaashoek. The Click modular router. *ACM Transactions on Computer Systems*, 18(3):263–297, 2000.

[75] S. Kounev and A. Buchmann. Improving data access of J2EE applications by exploiting asynchronous messaging and caching services. In *Proceedings of the 28th International Conference on Very Large Databases (VLDB'02)*, August 2002.

[76] D. Krishnamurthy and J. Rolia. Predicting the performance of an e-Commerce server: Those mean percentiles. In *Proceedings of the ACM SIGMETRICS Workshop on Internet Server Performance*, June 1998.

[77] D. Krishnamurthy, J. Rolia, and S. Majumdar. Synthetic workload generation for session-based systems. *In submission.* 2006.

[78] H. T. Kung and J. T. Robinson. On optimistic methods for concurrency control. *Transactions on Database Systems*, 6(2):213–226, 1981.

[79] A. Leff and J. T. Rayfield. Improving application throughput with Enterprise JavaBeans caching. In *Proceedings of the 23rd International Conference on Distributed Computing Systems (ICDCS'03)*, May 2003.

[80] A. Leff and J. T. Rayfield. Alternative edge-server architectures for enterprise JavaBeans applications. In *Proceedings of the 5th ACM/IFIP/USENIX International Middleware Conference*, October 2004.

[81] J. Lindfors, M. Fleury, and The JBoss Group. *JMX: Managing J2EE with Java Management Extensions*. SAMS, January 2002.

[82] D. Llambiri, A. Totok, and V. Karamcheti. Efficiently distributing component-based applications across wide-area environments. In *Proceedings of the 23rd International Conference on Distributed Computing Systems (ICDCS'03)*, May 2003.

[83] C. Lu, T. Abdelzaher, J. Stankovic, and S. Son. A feedback control approach for guaranteeing relative delays in web servers. In *Proceedings of the IEEE Real-Time Technology and Applications Symposium (RTAS'01)*, June 2001.

211

[84] V. Marangozova and D. Hagimont. An infrastructure for CORBA component replication. In *Proceedings of the First International IFIP/ACM Working Conference on Component Deployment (CD'02)*, June 2002.

[85] F. Marinescu. *EJB Design Patterns*. John Wiley & Sons, 2002.

[86] D. Menascé. Web server software architectures. *IEEE Internet Computing*, 7(6):78–81, 2003.

[87] D. Menascé, B. Abrahao, D Barbara, V. Almeida, and F. Ribeiro. Characterizing e-Business workloads using fractal methods. *Journal of Web Engineering*, 1(1):74–90, 2002.

[88] D. Menascé and V. Almeida. *Capacity Planning for Web Performance: Metrics, Models, and Methods*. Prentice Hall, 1998.

[89] D. Menascé, V. Almeida, R. Fonseca, and M. Mendes. A methodology for workload characterization of e-Commerce sites. In *Proceedings of the ACM Conference on Electronic Commerce*, November 1999.

[90] D. Menascé, V. Almeida, R. Riedi, Fl. Ribeiro, R. Fonseca, and W. Meira Jr. In search of invariants for e-Business workloads. In *Proceedings of the ACM Conference on Electronic Commerce*, October 2000.

[91] Microsoft Corporation. Component Object Model (COM) technologies. `http://www.microsoft.com/com/`.

[92] Microsoft Corporation. Microsoft .NET. `http://www.microsoft.com/net/`.

[93] New York University. Infrastructure for distributed deployment of Java EE applications. `http://www.cs.nyu.edu/~totok/professional/software/j2ee-deploy/j2ee-deploy.html`.

[94] M. H. Nodine and S. B. Zdonik. Cooperative transaction hierarchies: Transaction support for design applications. In *Proceedings of the 16th International Conference on Very Large Databases (VLDB'90)*, August 1990.

[95] Object Management Group. CORBA Component Model (CCM). http://www.omg.org/technology/documents/formal/components.htm.

[96] ObjectWeb Consortium. RUBiS: Rice University Bidding System. http://rubis.objectweb.org/.

[97] D. K. Pecaut, M. J. Silverstein, and P. Stanger. Winning the online consumer: Insights into online consumer behavior. *Boston Consulting Group*, March 2000. http://www.bcg.com.

[98] K. Petersen, M. J. Spreitzer, D. B. Terry, M. M. Theimer, and A. J. Demers. Flexible update propagation for weakly consistent replication. In *Proceedings of the 16th ACM Symposium on Operating Systems Principles (SOSP'97)*, October 1997.

[99] S. H. Phatak and B. R. Badrinath. Bounded locking for optimistic concurrency control. Rutgers University CS Technical Report DCS-TR-380, 1996.

[100] J. Pitkow. Summary of WWW characterizations. *World Wide Web Journal*, 2(1–2):3–13, 1999.

[101] K. Ramamritham and C. Pu. A formal characterization of epsilon serializability. *Knowledge and Data Engineering*, 7(6):997–1007, 1995.

[102] G. G. Roussas. *A Course in Mathematical Statistics*. Academic Press, 1997.

[103] B. Schroeder and M. Harchol-Balter. Web servers under overload: How scheduling can help. CMU Computer Science Technical Report CMU-CS-02-143, May 2002.

[104] P. Selvridge, B. Chaparro, and G. Bender. The World Wide Wait: Effects of delays on user performance. *International Journal of Industrial Ergonomics*, 29(1):15–20, 2001.

[105] D. Shasha, F. Llirbat, E. Simon, and P. Valduriez. Transaction chopping: Algorithms and performance studies. *ACM Transactions on Database Systems*, 20(3):325–363, 1995.

[106] W. Shi, K. Shah, Y. Mao, and V. Chaudhary. Tuxedo: a peer-to-peer caching system. In *Proceedings of the International Conference on Parallel and Distributed Processing Techniques and Applications (PDPTA'03)*, June 2003.

[107] W. Shi, R. Wright, E. Collins, and V. Karamcheti. Workload characterization of a personalized web site – and its implications for dynamic content caching. In *Proceedings of the 7th International Workshop on Web Caching and Content Distribution (WCW'02)*, August 2002.

[108] I. Singh, B. Stearns, M. Johnson, and the Enterprise Team. *Designing Enterprise Applications with the J2EE Platform*. Addison-Wesley, 2002.

[109] N. Singhmar, V. Mathur, V. Apte, and D. Manjunath. A combined LIFO-priority scheme for overload control of e-Commerce web servers. In *Proceedings of the International Survivability Workshop at IEEE-RTSS*, December 2004.

[110] L. Slothouber. A model of web server performance. In *Proceedings of the International World Wide Web Conference (WWW'96)*, May 1996.

[111] T. Stading, P. Maniatis, and M. Baker. Peer-to-peer caching schemes to address flash crowds. In *Proceedings of the 1st International Workshop on Peer-to-Peer Systems (IPTPS'02)*, March 2002.

[112] S. Stark and The JBoss Group. *JBoss Administration and Development*. JBoss Group, LLC, September 2002.

[113] C. Stewart and K. Shen. Performance modeling and system management for multi-component online services. In *Proceedings of the USENIX Symposium on Networked Systems Design and Implementation (NSDI'05)*, May 2005.

[114] Sun Microsystems. Enterprise JavaBeans (EJB) technology. http://java.sun.com/products/ejb/.

[115] Sun Microsystems. J2EE Connector Architecture (JCA). http://java.sun.com/j2ee/connector/.

[116] Sun Microsystems. Java Data Objects (JDO) technology. http://java.sun.com/products/jdo/.

[117] Sun Microsystems. Java Management Extensions (JMX). http://java.sun.com/products/JavaManagement/.

[118] Sun Microsystems. Java Message Service (JMS). http://java.sun.com/products/jms/.

[119] Sun Microsystems. Java Naming and Directory Interface (JNDI). http://java.sun.com/products/jndi/.

[120] Sun Microsystems. Java Pet Store sample J2EE application. http://java.sun.com/developer/releases/petstore/.

[121] Sun Microsystems. Java Platform Enterprise Edition (Java EE). http://java.sun.com/javaee/.

[122] Sun Microsystems. Java Remote Method Invocation (Java RMI). http://java.sun.com/products/jdk/rmi/.

[123] Sun Microsystems. Java Servlet Technology. http://java.sun.com/products/servlet/.

[124] Sun Microsystems. JavaServer Pages (JSP) technology. http://java.sun.com/products/jsp/.

[125] Sun Microsystems. JDBC technology. http://java.sun.com/products/jdbc/.

215

[126] C. Szyperski. *Component Software*. Addison-Wesley, 2002.

[127] Y. C. Tay, R. Suri, and N. Goodman. A mean value performance model for locking in databases: The no-waiting case. *Journal of the ACM*, 32(3):618–651, 1985.

[128] B. Tedeschi. Glitches in booking first class online, *The New York Times*, April 10, 2005, Travel Section, page 6.

[129] A. Thomasian. Two-phase locking performance and its thrashing behavior. *ACM Transactions on Database Systems*, 18(4):579–625, 1993.

[130] A. Thomasian. Concurrency control: Methods, performance, and analysis. *ACM Computing Surveys*, 30(1):70–119, 1998.

[131] A. Totok. RUBiS-NYU: A Session Facade design pattern implementation of the RUBiS Java EE benchmark application. New York University. http://www.cs.nyu.edu/~totok/professional/software/rubis/rubis.html.

[132] A. Totok. TPC-W-NYU: A Java EE implementation of the TPC-W benchmark. New York University. http://www.cs.nyu.edu/~totok/professional/software/tpcw/tpcw.html.

[133] Transaction Processing Performance Council. TPC-W: Transactional Web e-Commerce Benchmark. http://www.tpc.org/tpcw/.

[134] O. Ulusoy and G. G. Belford. Real-time transaction scheduling in database systems. *Information Systems*, 18(8):559–580, 1993.

[135] B. Urgaonkar, G. Pacifici, P. Shenoy, M. Spreitzer, and A. Tantawi. An analytical model for multi-tier Internet services and its applications. In *Proceedings of the ACM SIGMETRICS Conference on Measurement and Modeling of Computer Systems*, June 2005.

[136] B. Urgaonkar and P. Shenoy. Cataclysm: Handling extreme overloads in Internet services. In *Proceedings of the 23rd Annual ACM*

SIGACT-SIGOPS Symposium on Principles of Distributed Computing (PODC'04), July 2004.

[137] S. VanBoskirk, C. Li, and J. Parr. Keeping customers loyal. *Forrester Research*, May 2001. http://www.forrester.com.

[138] H. R. Varian. *Intermediate Microeconomics: A Modern Approach*. W. W. Norton & Company, Seventh edition, 2005.

[139] D. Villela, P. Pradhan, and D. Rubenstein. Provisioning servers in the application tier for e-Commerce systems. In *Proceedings of the 12th IEEE International Workshop on Quality of Service (IWQoS'04)*, June 2004.

[140] M. Wang, N.H. Chan, S. Papadimitriou, C. Faloutsos, and T. Madhyastha. Data mining meets performance evaluation: Fast algorithms for modeling bursty traffic. In *Proceedings of the 18th International Conference on Data Engineering (ICDE'02)*, February 2002.

[141] W. E. Weihl. Commutativity-based concurrency control for abstract data types. *IEEE Transactions on Computers*, 37(12):1488–1505, 1988.

[142] G. Weikum and G. Vossen. *Transactional Information Systems*. Morgan Kaufmann Publishers, 2002.

[143] T. Wilson. E-Biz bucks lost under SSL strain, *Internet Week Online*, May 20 1999.

[144] A. Wolman, G. M. Voelker, N. Sharma, N. Cardwell, A. Karlin, and H. M. Levy. On the scale and performance of cooperative web proxy caching. In *Proceedings of the 17th ACM Symposium on Operating Systems Principles (SOSP'99)*, December 1999.

[145] M. H. Wong and D. Agrawal. Tolerating bounded inconsistency for increasing concurrency in database systems. In *Proceedings of the 11th Symposium on Principles of Database Systems (PODS'92)*, June 1992.

[146] World Wide Web Consortium. Simple Object Access Protocol (SOAP). http://www.w3.org/TR/soap/.

[147] H. Yu and A. Vahdat. Design and evaluation of a continuous consistency model for replicated services. In *Proceedings of the 4th Symposium on Operating Systems Design and Implementation (OSDI'00)*, October 2000.

[148] Q. Zhang, E. Smirni, and G. Ciardo. Profit-driven service differentiation in transient environments. In *Proceedings of the 11th IEEE International Symposium on Modeling, Analysis, and Simulation of Computer and Telecommunications Systems (MASCOTS'03)*, October 2003.

[149] Z. L. Zhang, D. F. Towsley, and J. F. Kurose. Statistical analysis of generalized processor sharing scheduling discipline. *IEEE Journal on Selected Areas in Communications*, 13(6):1071–1080, 1995.

www.ingramcontent.com/pod-product-compliance
Lightning Source LLC
LaVergne TN
LVHW042333060326
832902LV00006B/149